animate FORM

animate FORM

GREG LYNN

artists
space
cardiff
bay opera
house
port
Authority
gateway
yokohama
port
Terminal
prototype
House
henle
onstad

PRINCETON
ARCHITECTURAL
PRESS

NEW YORK

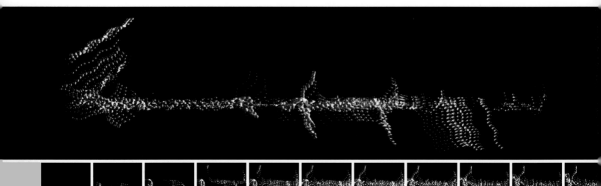

This project
has been made possible in part
through the generous support of
The Graham Foundation
for the Advancement of the Humanities

published by
Princeton Architectural Press
37 East Seventh Street,
New York, New York 10003, U.S.A.

© 1999 Greg Lynn
ISBN 1-56898-083-3
All rights reserved
04 03 02 01 00 99   4 3 2 1
Printed and bound in China

No part of this book or CD-ROM may be
reproduced in any manner without written
permission from the publisher except in
the context of reviews

Library of congress cataloging-in-
publication Data:
Lynn, Greg.
Animate form / Greg Lynn.
p. cm.
ISBN 1-56898-083-3 (hardcover)
1. Lynn, Greg--Exhibitions. I. Title.
NA737.L97A4 1998
720' .22'2--dc21   98-10076

project editor: Therese Kelly

book design: Greg Lynn, Ulrika Karlsson,
Heather Roberge, Andreas Froech

CD-ROM Design and production: Andreas
Froech, Dieter Janssen, Ed Keller

set in:
Gill Sans, Platelet

photo credits:
Jefferson Ellinger (Artists Space)
Andreas Froech (Henie Onstad)
Kim Holden (Yokohama study model)
David Joseph (Artists Space)
Gordon Kipping (Henie Onstad)
Hannes Strassl (stereolithography)

Every reasonable attempt has been made to
identify owners of copyright. Errors or
omissions will be corrected in subsequent
editions.

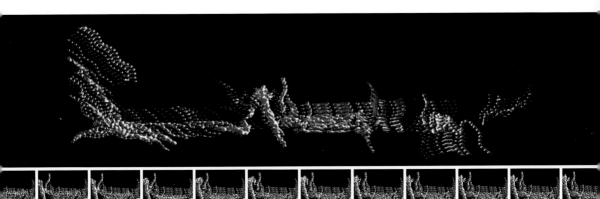

contents

To Catherine, for her support and insight, and to my parents, Jim and Dee.

animate form

Animation is a term that differs from, but is often confused with, **motion**. While motion implies movement and action, animation implies the evolution of a form and its shaping forces; it suggests animalism, animism, growth, actuation, vitality and virtuality.[1] In its manifold implications, animation touches on many of architecture's most deeply embedded assumptions about its structure. What makes animation so problematic for architects is that they have maintained an ethics of statics in their discipline. Because of its dedication to permanence, architecture is one of the last modes of thought based on the inert. More than even its traditional role of providing shelter, architects are expected to provide culture with stasis. This desire for timelessness is intimately linked with interests in formal purity and autonomy. Challenging these assumptions by introducing architecture to models of organization that are not inert will not threaten the essence of the discipline, but will advance it. Just as the development of calculus drew upon the historical mathematical developments that preceded it, so too will an animate approach to architecture subsume traditional models of statics into a more advanced system of dynamic organizations. Traditionally, in architecture, the abstract space of design is conceived as an ideal neutral space of Cartesian coordinates. In other design fields, however, design space is conceived as an environment of force and motion rather than as a neutral vacuum. In naval design, for example, the abstract space of design is imbued with the properties of flow, turbulence, viscosity, and drag so that the form of a hull can be conceived in motion through water. Although the form of a boat hull is designed to anticipate motion, there is no expectation that its shape will change. An ethics of motion neither implies nor precludes literal motion. Form can be shaped by the collaboration between an envelope and the active context in which it is situated. While physical form can be defined in terms of static coordinates, the virtual force of the environment in which it is designed contributes to its shape. The particular form of a hull stores multiple vectors of motion and flow from the space in which it was designed. A sailboat hull, for example, is designed to perform under multiple points of sail. For sailing downwind, the hull is designed as a planing surface. For sailing into the wind, the hull is designed to heal, presenting a greater surface area to the water. A boat hull does not change its shape when it changes its direction, obviously, but variable points of sail are incorporated into its surface. In this way, topology allows for not just the incorporation of a single moment but rather a multiplicity of vectors, and therefore, a multiplicity of times, in a single continuous surface.

Likewise, the forms of a dynamically conceived architecture may be shaped in association with virtual motion and force, but again, this does not mandate that the architecture change its shape. Actual movement often involves a mechanical paradigm of multiple discrete positions, whereas virtual movement allows form to occupy a multiplicity of possible positions continuously with the same form.

The term **virtual** has recently been so debased that it often simply refers to the digital space of computer-aided design. It is often used interchangeably with the term simulation. Simulation, unlike virtuality, is not intended as a diagram for a future possible concrete assemblage but is instead a visual substitute. "Virtual reality" might describe architectural design but as it is used to describe a simulated environment it would be better replaced by "simulated reality" or "substitute reality." Thus, use of the term virtual here refers to an abstract scheme that has the possibility of becoming actualized, often in a variety of possible configurations. Since architects produce drawings of buildings and not buildings themselves, architecture, more than any other discipline, is involved with the production of virtual descriptions.

There is one aspect of virtuality that architects have neglected, however, and that is the principle of virtual force and the differential variation it implies. Architectural form is conventionally conceived in a dimensional space of idealized stasis, defined by Cartesian fixed-point coordinates. An object defined as a vector whose trajectory is relative to other objects, forces, fields and flows, defines form within an active space of force and motion. This shift from a passive space of static coordinates to an active space of interactions implies a move from autonomous purity to contextual specificity.[2] Contemporary animation and special-effects software are just now being introduced as tools for design rather than as devices for rendering, visualization and imaging.[3]

The dominant mode for discussing motion in architecture has been the cinematic model, where the multiplication and sequencing of static snap-shots simulates movement. The problem with the motion-picture analogy is that architecture occupies the role of the static frame through which motion progresses. Force and motion are eliminated from form only to be reintroduced, after the fact of design, through concepts and techniques of optical procession.

In contrast, animate design is defined by the co-presence of motion and force at the moment of formal conception. Force is an initial condition, the cause of both motion and the particular inflections of a form. For example, in what is called "inverse kinematic" animation, the motion and shape of a form is defined by multiple interacting vectors that unfold in time perpetually and openly. With these techniques, entities are given vectorial properties before they are released into a space differentiated by gradients of force. Instead of a neutral abstract space for design, the context for design becomes an active abstract space that directs form within a current of forces that can be stored as information in the shape of the form. Rather than as a frame through which time and space pass, architecture can be modeled as a participant immersed within dynamical flows. In addition to the special-effects and animation industries, many other disciplines such as aeronautical design, naval design, and automobile design employ this animate approach to modeling form in a space that is a medium of movement and force.

Previous architectural experiments in capturing motion have involved the superimposition of simultaneous instances. The superimposition of a sequence of frames produces memory in the form of spatio-temporal simultaneity. This idea of an architecture in which time is built into form as memory has been a persistent theme throughout its history, but it was Siegfried Giedion in both *Mechanization Takes Command* (1948) and *Space, Time, and Architecture* (1941) who established these themes as the primary concern of twentieth-century

Figure 1:
Bucharest urban design competition study using particle animation flows to define variable densities across the site.

Figure 2:
Marcel Duchamp, *Nude Descending a Staircase, No. 2* (1912) Philadelphia Museum of Art, Louise and Walter Arensberg Collection.

Figure 3:
Umberto Boccioni, *Dynamism of a Soccer Player* (1913). Museum of Modern Art, New York, The Sidney and Harriet Janis Collection.

architectural theory and design.[4] Giedion included both cubist and futurist approaches to capturing motion in form, using as examples the work of Marcel Duchamp (fig. 2) and Umberto Boccioni (fig. 3). Giedion's interpretation of these cubo-futurist experiments continues to influence contemporary design and theory.[5] In both approaches, multiple static frames of an object in time are captured and superimposed in the same space simultaneously, generating a temporal palimpsest.

Another model of indexical time is associated with Colin Rowe and his disciples. In Rowe's text, "Transparency: Literal and Phenomenal," co-authored with Robert Slutzky, the idea of a formal, or phenomenal, transparency is proposed along with literal transparency.[6] Phenomenal transparency is the tracing or imprinting of a deeper formal space on a surface. Similarly, examples of formal or phenomenal time include "*shearing*," "*shifting*," and "*rotating*" operations. Superimposed snap-shots of motion imply time as a phenomenal movement between frames or moments. For instance, Kenneth Frampton's description of Charles Gwathmey's early work as "*rotational*" is one such example of time being used to describe the movement between superimposed, formal moments.[7] Another example is that of the "*trace*," a term that has emerged in the last twenty years as a graphical notation of time and motion in architecture.[8] In such projects, a design process of sequential formal operations is recorded in the building's configuration through colors, alignments, imprints, additions and subtractions. One such example is the simultaneous presence of multiple historical ground conditions at a single moment. The intervals between the moments that are superimposed generate irresolute conditions which are exploited for their destabilizing effect on the present.

In all of these indexical responses to time, a superimposition or sequence of static forms is put into relation such that the viewer resolves multiple states through the initiation of optical motion. Although form is thought in series and motion in these examples, movement is something that is added back to the object by the viewer. This involves a dialectic definition of motion that assumes that matter is inert while our experience of it involves movement. Statics becomes the condition of matter without force and dynamics becomes the condition of matter acted on by force. Both positions assume that force is something which can be added or subtracted from matter.

The modeling of architecture in a conceptual field populated by forces and motion contrasts with these previous paradigms and technologies of formal stasis. Stasis is a concept which has been intimately linked with architecture in at least five important ways, including 1) permanence, 2) usefulness, 3) typology, 4) procession, and 5) verticality. However, statics does not hold an essential grip on architectural thinking as much as it is a lazy habit or default that architects either choose to reinforce or contradict for lack of a better model. Each of these assumptions can be transformed once the virtual space in which architecture is conceptualized is mobilized with both time and force. With the example of permanence, the dominant cultural expectation is that buildings must be built for eternity when in fact most buildings are built to persist for only a short time. Rather than designing for permanence, techniques for obsolescence, dismantling, ruination, recycling and abandonment through time warrant exploration. Another characteristic of static models is that of functional fixity. Buildings are often assumed to have a particular and fixed relationship to their programs, whether they are intersected, combined or even flexibly programmed. Typological fixity, of the kind promoted by Colin Rowe for instance, depends on a closed static order to underlie a family of continuous variations. This concept of a discrete, ideal, and fixed prototype can be subsumed by the model of the numerically controlled multi-type that is flexible, mutable, and differential. This multi-type, or **performance envelope**, does not privilege a fixed type but instead models a series of relationships or expressions between a range of potentials. Similarly, independent interacting variables can be linked to influence one another through logical expressions defining the size, position, rotation, direction, or speed of an object by looking to other objects for their characteristics. This concept of an envelope of potential from which either a single or a series of **instances** can be taken, is radically different from the idea of a fixed prototype that can be varied.

Finally, static models underwrite the retrograde understanding of gravity as a simple, unchanging, vertical force. Architecture remains as the last refuge for members of the flat-earth society. The relationships of structure to force and gravity are by definition multiple and interrelated, yet architects tend to reduce these issues to what is still held as a central truth: that buildings stand up vertically. In fact, there are multiple interacting structural pressures exerted on buildings from many directions, including lateral wind loads, uplift, shear, and earthquakes, to name a few of the non-vertical conditions. Any one of these **live** loads could easily exceed the relative weight of the building and its vertical **dead** loads. The naive understanding of structure as primarily a problem of the vertical transfer of dead gravity loads to the ground excludes, for instance, the fact that lighter buildings have a tendency to uplift; the main structural concern in these cases is how to tether the roof. Of course architects and structural engineers do not ignore these other structural factors, but the primary perception of structure has always been that it should be vertical. A reconceptualization of ground and verticality in light of complex vectors and movements might not change the expediency and need for level floors, but it would open up possibilities for structure and support that take into account orientations other than the simply vertical.

These concerns are not merely technical as architecture presently expresses also the cultural diagrams of stasis. Despite the popular conception among architects that gravity is a fact, the contemporary debates about theories of gravity could inform present discussions of architecture in the same spirit that they have done in the past. The history of theories of gravity are extremely nuanced, fascinating and unresolved. Since the time of Sir Isaac Newton, gravity has been accepted as the mutual relative attraction of masses in space. Given a constant mass, stability is achieved through orbits rather than stasis. This distinction between stasis and orbital or dynamic stability is important. In the case of a single, simple gravity, **stasis** is the ordering system through the unchanging constant force of a ground point. In the case of a more complex concept of gravity, mutual attraction generates motion; **stability** is the ordering of motion into rhythmic phases. In the simple, static model of gravity, motion is eliminated at the beginning. In the complex, stable model of gravity, motion is an ordering principle. Likewise, discreteness, timelessness, and fixity are characteristic of stasis; multiplicity, change, and development are characteristic of stability.

These differences are very apparent in the two models of gravity debated by René Descartes and Gottfried Wilhelm Leibniz. Descartes isolated and reduced elements in a dynamic system to their constitutive identities to create a steady-state equation: he eliminated time and force from the equation in order to calculate a precise position. Leibniz, on the other hand, examined components within their contextual field of influences and within a developing temporal continuum. By retaining the creative structural role of time and force, Leibniz determined that a position in space can only be calculated continuously as a vectoral flow.[9] The name that he attributed to any provisionally reduced component or primitive element is that of the "*monad*." Where Newton used calculus to replace the zero value of statics with a "*derivative*," Leibniz formulated the concept of the "*integral,*" where within any monad there is a kernel of the whole equation in the form of the variables. Any monad has the ability to unfold a "*possible world*." Thus integral calculus is structured on a monad logic of continuous multiplicity. The shift from a discrete model of gravity as a force that could be eliminated from matter, to a concept of gravity as integral and continuous with masses in space, involves a redefinition of space from being neutral and timeless to being temporally dynamic. Once design is posed within a Leibnizian monadological space, architecture may embrace a sensibility of micro and macro contextual specificity as a logic that can not be idealized in an abstract space of fixed coordinates. In such an abstract active space, the statics of fixed points in neutral space is replaced by the stability of vectors that balance one another in a phase space.

If architecture is to approach this more complex concept of gravity, its design technologies should also incorporate factors of time and motion. Throughout the history of architecture, descriptive techniques have impacted the way in which architectural design and construction has been practiced. In the eighteenth century, the orrery (fig. 4) came to represent not only the image of the machine but also the conceptual processes of a universe that is harmonically regulated as a closed system of circular orbits around radial center points. Because an orrery uses fixed radial points, any discrete moment in time can be calculated as a fixed point. The compass, like the orrery, has implicit in it a series of conceptual and disciplinary limits that are rehearsed with every arc that is drawn. Events such as the advent of perspective, stereometric projection, and other geometric techniques have extended the descriptive repertoire of architectural designers.

15

 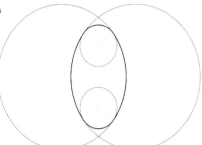 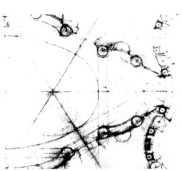

In our present age, the virtual space within which architecture is conceived is now being rethought by the introduction of advanced motion tools and a constellation of new diagrams based on the computer. The geometry and the mathematics that Leibniz invented to describe this interactive, combinatorial, and multiplicitous gravity remain as the foundations for topology and calculus upon which contemporary animation technology is based. There can be little doubt that the advent of computer-aided visualization has allowed architects to explore calculus-based forms for the first time.

The sequential continuity of more than two variables interacting with one another poses a problem that only calculus can answer. First posed by Karl Weierstrass, Charles Hermite and Gosta Mittag-Lefler in 1885, the "n-body" problem was later made famous by Henri Poincare in 1889, when he was able to prove that no discrete solution for such a problem could exist. The fundamental aspect of this problem, referred to as "the Poincare three-body problem," is that the temporal and spatial position of entities cannot be mathematically calculated for a future position without sequentially calculating the positions leading up to that moment. The mathematics of form and space that architects have historically understood, involve mathematical descriptions from which time has been eliminated. In the three-body problem however, time, or more properly duration and sequence, are integral to the spatial relationships being calculated. Another aspect of this kind of relationship in which three or more objects interact, is that they often produce nonlinear behavior. The method by which these problems can be calculated is through a mathematics that is sequential and continuous: thus the invention by both Newton and Leibniz of differential calculus.

Although the mechanical, acoustic, and structural systems of buildings have been calculated and conceived using the tools of calculus, architects infrequently use calculus for the design of form. The fact that architecture is so heavily dependent on mathematics for the description of space has been a

Figure 4:
Reproduction of the apparatus commissioned by Charles Boyle, 4th Earl of Cork and Orrery, showing the relative positions and motions of bodies in the solar system by balls moved by wheelwork. Reproduction by Van Cort Instruments, Inc.

Figure 5:
An elipse constructed with four circles with four radii. The connecting lines between the radii become the points of tangency where the composite curves change from being defined in relation to one radius to another.

Figure 6:
Plan detail of Borromini's sketch for "Quattro Fontane" Church of San Carlo, showing the use of complex composite curves construced out of linked segments of circles and spheres. From Anthony Blunt, *Vita e opere di Borromini* (Rome: Editori Laterza, 1983), 51.

Figure 7:
A ceiling detail of the cupola of Borromini's "Quattro Fontane." From Anthony Blunt, *Vita e opere di Borromini* (Rome: Editori Laterza, 1983), 51.

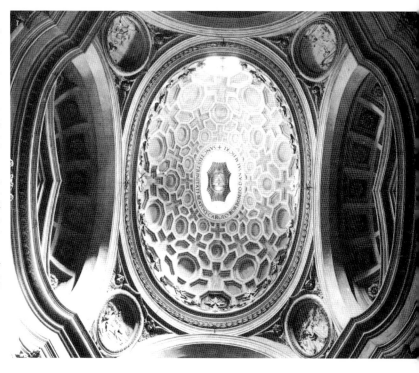

stumbling block to the use of motion and flow in the design process, as these ideas require that architects draw geometries whose underlying mathematics is calculus. The tools that architects use to draw, such as adjustable triangles and compasses, are based on simple algebra. The prevalence of topological surfaces in even the simplest CAD software, along with the ability to tap the time-and-force modeling attributes of animation software, presents perhaps the first opportunity for architects to draw and sketch using calculus. The challenge for contemporary architectural theory and design is to try to understand the appearance of these tools in a more sophisticated way than as simply a new set of shapes. Issues of force, motion and time, which have perennially eluded architectural description due to their "*vague essence,*" can now be experimented with by supplanting the traditional tools of exactitude and stasis with tools of gradients, flexible envelopes, temporal flows and forces.[10]

As architects have been disciplined to eliminate questions of flow and motion from the rigorous description of space, these qualities have been relegated to personal taste and casual definition. Because of the present lack of experience and precedent with issues of motion and force in archi-

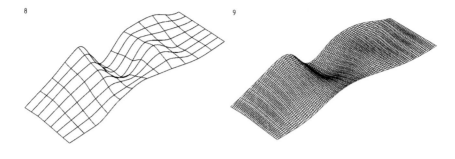

8   9

Figure 8:
A spline surface drawn with vectors that hang from points.

Figure 9:
The spline surface after being converted to triangular polygons.

tecture, these issues might best be raised from within the technological regimes of the tools rather than from within architectural history.[11] Through experimentation with non-architectural regimes, architects may discover how to engage time and motion in design. The computer has already proven to be useful as both a descriptive and a visualizing tool to architects, but the introduction of time and motion techniques into architecture is not simply a visual phenomenon. The visual qualities of computer-generated images may be important but it seems misguided to understand geometry in terms of style. The invention of stylistic categories risks the reproduction of the same spurious comparisons of modern architecture to boats and aircraft based on the similarity of shapes. For instance, although geodesic domes often employ triangulated surfaces and some computer programs convert vector surfaces to fixed points through the use of triangular polygon meshes (figs. 8 and 9), it is a very shallow comparison to equate architecture designed using topological surfaces to Buckminster Fuller simply because of the commonality of triangulated surfaces.[12]

Nonetheless, there are distinct formal and visual consequences of the use of computer animation. For instance, the most obvious aesthetic consequence is the shift from volumes defined by Cartesian coordinates to topological surfaces defined by U and V vector coordinates (fig. 12). Another obvious aesthetic byproduct of these spatial models is the predominance of deformation and transformation techniques available in a time-based system of flexible surfaces (fig. 13). These are not merely shapes but the expression of the mathematics of the topological medium.

In addition to the aesthetic and material consequences of computer-generated forms, computer software also offers capabilities as a conceptual and organizational tool. But because of the stigma and fear of releasing control of the design process to software, few architects have attempted to use the computer as a schematic, organizing and generative medium for design. The limits and tendencies of this tool, as a medium for design, must be clearly understood conceptually before they can be grasped by a systematic intuition.[13]

There are also some misconceptions about the role of computers in the design process. A precious few architectural designers and theorists, Karl Chu and John Frazier being the most lucid among them, argue for the creative capacity of computers to facilitate genetic design strategies. The genetic, or rule-based, phenomenon of computation should not be discounted. Yet at the same time, genetic processes should not be equated with either intelligence or nature. The computer is not a brain. Machine intelligence might best be described as that of mindless connections. When connecting multiple variables, the computer simply connects them, it does not think critically about how it connects. The present limits of connectionism are staggeringly complex, and the directness with which multiple entities can be related challenges human sensibility. The response has been to attempt to develop a commensurate sensibility in the machines themselves; but the failures of artificial intelligence suggest a need to develop a systematic human intuition about the connective medium, rather than attempting to build criticality into the machine. Even in the most scientific applications of computer simulations it is argued that first an intuition must be developed in order to recognize the nonlinear behavior of computer simulations.[14] Also, the computer is not nature. Although it makes shapes that are temporally and formally open to deformation and inflection, those shapes are not organic. The organic appearance of what will later be discussed as a system of interaction and curvilinearity is a result of organizational principles based on differentials. The formal organizations that result from the sequential mathematical calculation of differential equations are irreducibly open in terms of their shape. They are often interpreted as organic because of the inability to reduce these shapes to an ideal form. In contrast, the reducible, fixed forms of simple mathematics—such as spheres, cubes, pyramids, cones and cylinders—have a simplicity and purity that allows them to transcend their formal particularities.

Instead of approaching the computer as either a brain or nature, the computer might be considered as a pet. Like a pet, the computer has already been domesticated and pedigreed, yet it does not behave with human intelligence. Just as a pet introduces an element of wildness to our domestic habits that must be controlled and disciplined, the computer brings both a degree of discipline and unanticipated behavior to the design process. By negotiating the degree of discipline and wildness, one can cultivate an intuition into the behavior of computer-aided design systems and the mathematics behind them.

There are three fundamental properties of organization in a computer that are very different from the characteristics of inert mediums such as paper and pencil: **topology**, **time**, and **parameters**. These three properties should be discussed, beginning with the principles of topological entities, continuing with the implications that topological forms raise for the relationship between time and shape, and concluding with a discussion of statistics and parameters that can be stored in these timed surfaces.

One of the first principles of topological entities is that because they are defined with calculus they take the shape of a multiplicity; meaning they are not composed of discrete points but rather, they are composed of a continuous stream of relative values. Historically, baroque geometries of composite entities, such as multiple radii, have been cited as multiplicitous spaces. But the idea that the baroque period anticipates topology in architecture is somewhat misplaced. There is a critical difference between the discrete geometry of baroque space—a geometry of multiple points, and the continuity of topology—a multiplicity without points. Where baroque space is defined by multiple radii, a topological surface is defined as a flow that hangs from fixed points that are weighted. Although baroque space is geometrically highly continuous and highly differentiated, it does retain multiple spatial centers. The continuous contours of baroque interiors are composed of segments of multiple discrete radial elements (figs. 5 and 10). For example, in Francesco Borromini's Quattro Fontane the complex of primitive volumes is tangentially aligned to produce a continuous surface, giving the space simultaneous dynamism and centrality (figs. 6 and 7). The relationships between these radial primitives are often of bilaterally symmetry and always of tangency.

Instead of being defined by points and centers, topology is characterized by flexible surfaces composed of splines (fig. 11). These splines are oriented in an opposing U and V orientation to construct surfaces composed of curve networks (fig. 19). Unlike lines, splines are vectors defined with direction. The vectors are suspended from lines with hanging weights similar to the geometry of a catenoidal curve.[15] Yet unlike a catenoidal curve, a spline can accommodate weights and gravities directed in free space. The points, or "*control vertices*," from which these weights hang, and through which the

10

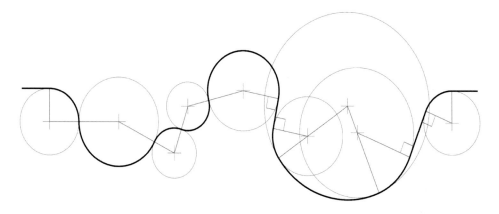

Figure 10:
An example of a composite curve using the same logic of regional definition and tangency as the ellipse described in Figure 5. Each section of the composite curve is defined by a fixed radius. The connection between radial curve segments occurs at points of tangency that are defined by a line connecting the radii. Perpendicular to theses lines, straight line segments can be inserted between the radial curves.

11

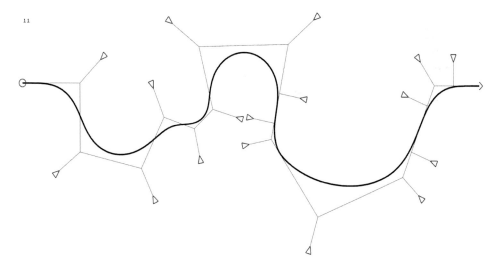

Figure 11:
A similar curve described using spline geometry, in which the radii are replaced by control vertices with weights and handles through which the curved spline flows.

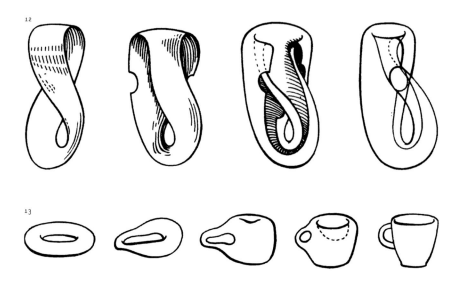

12

13

Figure 12:
A spline surface that begins as a twisted mobius band and is stretched and joined along its edges to form a self-inter-secting surface. Enclosed volumes are trapped within the surface by both the joining and intersecting operations. From Stephen Barr, *Experiments in Topology* (New York: Dover Publications, Inc., 1964), 69.

Figure 13:
A transformation of a ring into a cup through the flexibility of a single surface. From Stephen Barr, *Experiments in Topology* (New York: Dover Publications, Inc., 1964), 4.

spline flows, are located in X, Y, Z coordinate space. From a sequence of control vertices the direction and strength of weights establishes a tension along the hulls. Although the control vertices, hulls, and weights are defined in a point-based, Cartesian, space, the splines are not defined as points but as flows. The spline curve is unlike a line or radius in that its shape is not reducible to exact coordinates. The spline curve flows as a stream between a constellation of weighted control vertices and any position along this continuous series can only be defined relative to its position in the sequence. The formal character of a particular spline is based on the number of control vertices influencing a particular region of the flow. For instance, a three-degree spline (fig. 14) will begin at its root and determine its inflection between every three points in a series. A seven-degree spline curve (fig. 15) will be defined by groups of seven control vertices, thus appearing smoother. A two-degree spline (fig. 16) will appear linear because it lacks smooth continuity between control vertices. Even though the control vertices remain constant in these examples, the particular shape changes due to the degree of relative definition of the controlling points of the sequential flow. Similarly, without changing the position of any one of the control vertices or the degree of the spline, the shape will be altered when the weight or direction of any of the normals is altered (fig. 18).

A change in any point distributes an inflection across regions of these entities. Because splines are vectorial flows through sequences of points they are by definition continuous multiplicities rather than discrete entities. A multiplicity is a collection of components that is neither reducible to a single entity nor to a collection of multiple entities. A multiplicity is neither one nor many, but a continuous assemblage of heterogeneous singularities that exhibits both collective qualities of continuity and local qualities of heterogeneity. In the use of topology in design, these multiplicities imply a very different approach to location, as there are no discrete points along a spline.

The two linked principles that are central to the temporal component of topology are (1) the immanent curvatures that result from the combinatorial logic of differential equations and (2) the mathematical cause of that curvature. Because topological entities are based on vectors, they are capable of systematically incorporating time and motion into their shape as inflection. Inflection, or continuous curvature is the graphical and mathematical model for the imbrication of multiple forces in time. The shift from linearity to curvilinearity is a feature of contemporary mathematics and geometry that has been discussed elsewhere.[16] Curvilinearity is a more sophisticated and complex form of organization than linearity in two regards: (1) it integrates multiple rather than single entities, and (2) it is capable of expressing vectorial attributes, and therefore time and motion. Curvature in a temporal environment is the method by which the interaction of multiple forces can be structured, analyzed, and expressed.

The calculation of time as expressed through curvature is possible with calculus, which animates numerical snapshots at an infinite speed, simulating time. Underlying all of the contemporary animation software is a mathematics of the infinitely small interval which simulates actual motion and time through **keyframing**. These transformations can be linearly **morphed** or they can involve nonlinear interactions through **dynamics**. These sequential transformations are possible because the formal entities themselves are described using flexible topological surfaces made of vector splines rather than points.

An example of curvature as a mathematical and intuitive system can be explained by the situation of a Frisbee™ being chased by a running dog. There are at least three contributing elements to the path of the dog and its possible intersection with the projectile. First, the Frisbee™ has a vec-

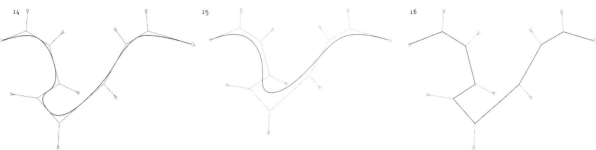

Figure 14:
A three-degree spline, where the curvature and inflection is determined by a sequence of positions of three points along the motion flow of the spline. The spline is constructed from control vertices, connected in a sequence, and from which a vector curve hangs with a directional flow.

Figure 15:
A seven-degree spline, where the curvature and inflection is determined by a sequence of positions of seven adjacent points along the path of the spline. The seven-degree spline is therefore much smoother than the three-degree spline because it interpolates between a greater number of adjacent points.

Figure 16:
A two-degree spline, where the curvature and inflection is determined by a sequence of positions between only two points along the motion flow of the spline. The spline therefore appears to be a poly-line.

tor for direction and speed; second, the space in which they move has a wind velocity and direction as well; and third, the Frisbee™ has a gravitational attraction to the earth. In order to intersect with the Frisbee™ at a future moment in time, the dog will not follow the projectile but perform a differential equation to calculate both its and the Frisbee's™ future positions in time as vectors moving toward a moment of possible intersection. The path of the dog will inevitably be described by a curved line. The inflections of this curved line indicate the velocities, directions and timing of each of the imbricated vectors. This situation cannot be described by a straight line with endpoints because, mathematically, it is a differential equation with more than two interacting components. Likewise, any multiplicity such as this will be described by some form of curvature because multiplicities are constructed of interacting entities exerting a differential influence on one another. Curvature is a mode of integrating complex interacting entities into a continuous form. What is important about this example is that initially, the hypothetical dog might be expected to duplicate the trajectory of the Frisbee™ and therefore it would have difficulty catching the moving object. With practice, the dog might be expected to intuit the patterns of motion of the Frisbee™ and eventually it will follow a cut-off path in order to intersect with the Frisbee™. Although the dog does not actually calculate a differential equation, it perceives the motion patterns of multiple vector fields acting in space and time and can antici-

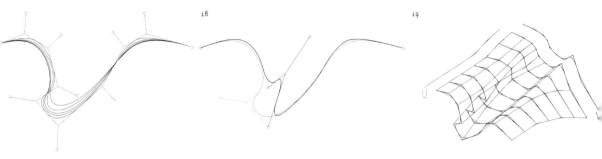

Figure 17:
A superimposed series of splines sharing the same control vertices with different degrees of influence; a two-, three-, four-, five-, six-, and seven-degree spline curve.

Figure 18:
Two splines showing the distributed effect of a change in one control vertex across the length of the spline. The fourth control vertex is moved and its weight is increased. This change is distributed along the length of the spline rather than only between fixed points.

Figure 19:
A spline surface, or mesh, constructed out of groups of splines whose control vertices are connected across one another. The splines are grouped into U and V directions, where the control vertices of the U direction splines pass through the control vertices of the V direction splines.

pate the unfolding of these patterns. By analogy, it is not necessary for architects to perform the differential equations that generate topological forms, as the equation for even the simplest spline is too complex for most architects to calculate. Instead, designers must understand the patterns of topology as they unfold dynamically with varying performance, rather than understanding them merely as shapes.

The shapes that are formed in computer-aided design are the result of decisions made using parameters. Numerical data which describe characteristics of the virtual design environment—such as temperature, gravity, and other forces—have an impact on the forms which result. For example, dynamic modeling systems are based on the interaction of multiple parameter statements calculated sequentially rather than in an instant. Numerical parameters can be keyframed and dynamically linked through **expressions** to alter the shape of objects. In addition to mere changes in shape, these parameters control gradient characteristics of fields such as directional forces, gravities, warps, and particles. Gradient parameters of decay, wave behavior, attraction, and density affect objects as numerical fields of force rather than as object transformations. The linkages between these characteristics of time, topology, and parameters combine to establish the virtual possibilities for designing in an animate rather than static space. Each of these characteristics can be used to rethink the familiar

Cartesian space of neutral equilibrium as a more active space of motion and flow.

The curvilinearity which results from these multiple parameters has previously been simplistically understood as a debased form of linearity, but in fact, it is the ordering of a dynamical system of differential factors. In the early part of this century, Scottish zoolologist Sir D'Arcy Thompson analyzed variations in the morphology of animals using deformable grids, which yielded curvilinear lines due to changes in form (fig. 20). He compared the curvature of deformations in formal configurations to the curvature of statistical data, such as speed, temperature, and weight. Thompson was one of the first scientists to notate **gradient** forces (such as temperature) through **deformation**, **inflection**, and **curvature**.[17] These three terms all involve the registration of force on form. Rather than thinking of deformation as a subset of the pure, the term deformation can be understood as a system of regulation and order that proceeds through the integration and resolution of multiple interacting forces and fields.

Where Thompson pioneered the analyses of deformation as an index of contextual forces acting on an organism, in the late nineteenth century Étienne-Jules Marey pioneered the study of curvature as the notation of both force and time. Francois Dagognet described the project of Marey as

> . . . showing what one could learn from a curve, which was not merely a simple 'reproduction.' It was from and with the curve that forces could initially be calculated. It was easy to obtain the mass of the body as well as the speed it was going (chronobiology); from this one could induce the force that had set it in motion, the work expended to produce this action. The trajectory always had to be questioned and interpreted. Not only were the slightest nicks and notches in the line due to certain factors, but they enabled the determination of resistances as well as impulses.[18]

Marey was one of the first morphologists to move from the study of form in inert Cartesian space, devoid of force and motion, to the study of rhythms, movements, pulses, and flows and their effects on form. These factors he termed "*motor evidence.*" In his book *Animal Mechanism* he shifted his attention from the study of internal pulses and rhythms to the external movements of animals. Unlike Muybridge and others who also employed chronophotography techniques, Marey triggered the exposures with both pneumatic and electrical sensors located on the animals (fig. 21). This, along with his method of attaching tiny reflecting optical disks allowed Marey to sequence the exposures with rhythms of motion (fig. 22). Dagognet describes Marey as pursuing "*movements not moments*" in his continuous

Figure 20:
Study of the transformation of crustacean carapaces through the deformation of a flexible grid or "rubber mat" by D'Arcy Thompson. From Thompson, *On Growth and Form, The Complete Revised Edition* (New York: Dover Publications, Inc., 1992), 1057.

Figure 21:
Étienne-Jules Marey used pneumatic triggers, attached to the joints of animals, to trigger camera exposures in rhythmic sequences. In this way, the rhythm of photographic instances were sequenced to the movements of the animal. "Device for harnessing the pigeon to the revolving frame," from Marey, "Le Vol des oiseaux," as appears in François Dagognet, *Étienne-Jules Marey: A Passion for the Trace* (New York: Zone Books, 1992), 85.

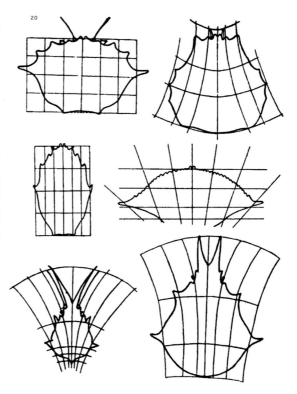

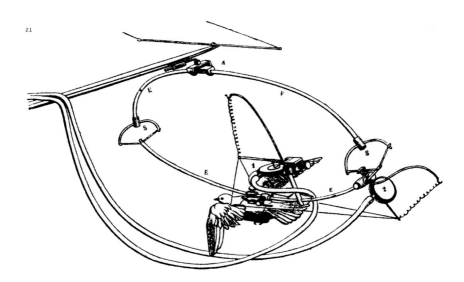

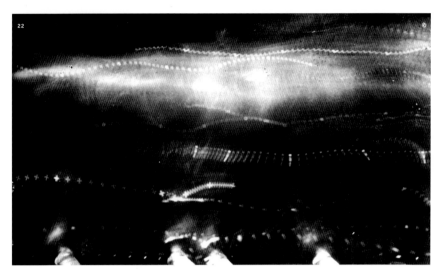

Figure 22:
Marey used reflective optical disks attached to key points of the body to capture points of motion. In this example of a horse walking, the film is exposed at a rate where the points begin to blur into motion trails. "Oscillations of the front limb of the horse walking," from Marey, "Le Vol des oiseaux," as appears in François Dagognet, *Étienne-Jules Marey: A Passion for the Trace* (New York: Zone Books, 1992), 75.

data recordings. After exposing rhythmic sequences of images on a single plate, Marey would connect curved lines through these points to describe a continuity across the snapshots (fig. 23). To borrow a term used to describe the behavior of chaotic attractors, Marey produced "*phase portraits*" by describing time as a continuous curvilinear flow, rather than a divisible sequence reducible to discrete frames. This is the critical difference between Marey's traces of vector movement and the techniques of sequential traces. Marey's model for continuous time based on the inflection and curvature of motion paths and flows, is akin to computer animation.

LANDSCAPE

In addition to these examples of analyzing time, movement, and transformation, another model that has been developed in conjunction with evolutionary theories is the idea of the fitness landscape. With the replacement of fixed types by temporally organized phylogenetic trees, came the model of the developmental landscape to describe the space within which organisms evolve. In mathematics the landscape model has been developed by Rene Thom, in physics by Stuart Kauffman and in developmental biology by Conrad Waddington. It initially appeared when Francis Galton described evolution in terms of a fitness landscape; whereby a surface represents an external environment across which a facetted sphere rolled. The facetted sphere represents an organism with its own internal constraints, and the

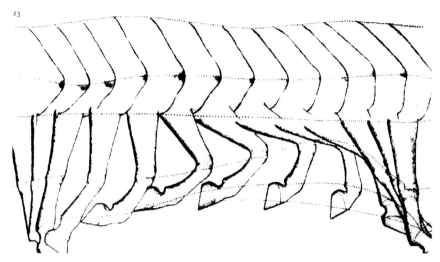

23

Figure 23:
Marey would connect curved lines through these points to describe a curvilinear continuity across the snapshots. "Oscillations of the front limb of the horse galloping," from Marey, "Le Vol des oiseaux," as appears in François Dagognet, *Étienne-Jules Marey: A Passion for the Trace* (New York: Zone Books, 1992), 75.

landscape represents its potential pathways of development. This concept of a landscape of development informed Charles Darwin's evolutionary theory of speciation. Similar to any landscape model of organization is an evolutionary or developmental logic.

A landscape is a system where a point change is distributed smoothly across a surface so that its influence cannot be localized at any discrete point. Splines are the constituent element of topological landscapes. Spline surfaces have already been explained as vector sequences whose regions of inflection produce singularities on a continuous surface. The slow undulations that are built into any landscape surface as hills and valleys do not mobilize space through action but instead through implied virtual motion. The movement of a point across a landscape becomes the collaboration of the initial direction, speed, elasticity, density, and friction of the object along with the inflections of the landscape across which it is traveling. The landscape can initiate movements across itself without literally moving. The inflections of a landscape present a context of gradient slopes which are enfolded into its shape. The condition of oriented surfaces has been elaborated by Paul Virilio and Claude Parent in terms of "*oblique*" movement.[19] Likewise, any object moving across a landscape has an initial condition of speed and density that is unfolded across the landscape. This collaboration of enfolding a context and unfolding an object is a temporal, mobile, and

LANDSCAPE STORING POTENTIAL MOVEMENT

combinatorial model for stability and organization. In this schema the object has actual force and motion, where the landscape has virtual force and motion stored in its slopes. The slope of a landscape is a gradient of motion, direction, and time. A landscape also implies a geological time-scale of formation in that although it appears static at any instant, its form is the product of long historical processes of development. This class of landscape objects can be extended to include any form from which temporal development cannot be simply reduced. Topological surfaces that store force in the inflections of their shape behave as landscapes in that the slopes that are generated store energy in the form of oriented rather than neutral surfaces.

The earlier example of the boat hull is itself a micro-landscape for the movements stored in its surface shapes, across which viscous water flows. Similarly the global flows of the water and wind present a macro-landscape for the motion of the boat to flow through. Other topological landscapes include isomorphic polysurfaces (or **blobs**), **skeletons** (or inverse kinematics networks), **warps**, **forces**, and **particles**. Spline entities are intensively influenced by their context due to the fact that they are defined by hanging weights, gravity, and force. For example, the weights and directions pulling on control vertices in space can be affected by gradients of attractive or repulsive force in which the spline is situated. Similarly, the weights of one spline surface can effect those of another spline surface (figs. 24 and 25). These resulting structures are called blobs for their ability to mutually inflect one another and form composite assemblages. The blob is an alternative example of a topological surface exhibiting landscape characteristics although it does not look like a topography. These blob assemblages are neither multiple nor single, neither internally contradictory nor unified. Their complexity involves the fusion of multiple elements into an assemblage that behaves as a singularity while remaining irreducible to any single simple organization. With isomorphic polysurfaces, "meta-clay," "meta-ball," or "blob" models, the geometric objects are defined as monadlike primitives with internal forces of attraction and mass. A blob is defined with a center, a surface area, a mass relative to other objects, and a field of influence. The field of influence defines a relational zone within which the blob will fuse with, or be inflected by, other blobs. When two or more linked blob objects are proximate they will either (1) mutually redefine their respective surfaces based on their particular gravitational properties or (2) actually fuse into one contiguous surface defined by the interactions of their respective centers and zones of inflection and fusion.

Because it is not reducible to any single simple ordering principle, a blob's fusion and unification are distinct from a discrete totality or whole. In the

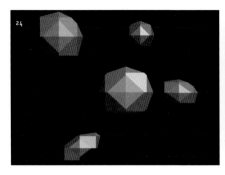 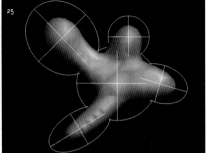

Figure 24:
Disconnected primitives used to compose an isomorphic polysurface.

Figure 25:
Isomorphic polysurface with primitives fused into a single surface.

case of the isomorphic polysurfaces, either a low number of interacting components or a regular distribution of components will yield a global form that is more or less simple. On the other hand, a high number of components and an irregular distribution of those components yields a global form that is more or less complex. The difference between simple and complex systems is relative to the number of interactions between components. In this schema, there is no essential difference between a more or less spherical formation and a blob. The sphere and its provisional symmetries are merely the index of a rather low level of interactions, while the blob is an index of a high degree of information, where information is equated with difference. Thus, even what seems to be a sphere is actually a blob without influence; an inexact form that merely masquerades as an exact form because it is isolated from adjacent forces. Yet, as a blob, it is capable of fluid and continuous differentiation based on interactions with neighboring forces with which it can be either inflected or fused. In this way, complexity is always present as potential in even the most simple or primitive of forms. Moreover, it is measured by the degrees of both continuity and difference that are copresent at any moment.

Like a natural landscape that stores the history of its geological formation in its shape, these fused topological aggregates manifest their geological conglomeration on a single surface. Time, force, and multiplicity constitute the form of a geological landscape. This structuring of time and energy through curvilinear inflections is characteristic of motion or action geom-

etry. These inflections index both the internal combinations and relationships of elements and their deformation within a larger contextual field.
When proposing the model of an internally regulated structure, there are
two possibilities: the first approach posits an essential internal order that
can be discovered through reductive analysis, the second is a loose binding
of constraints that can be realigned and reconfigured in a proliferative and
evolutionary manner. In the second category, the internal order is both
activated and made legible through the unfolding of its order instigated by
external forces. The relationship between a system of internal constraints,
such as skeletons (inverse kinematic chains), particles, or blobs and the
context in which they unfold is intensive. Just as a topological landscape or
an assemblage of blobs stores various attractions and combinations in a single surface, so too can topological entities be mutually inflected by the
fields in which they are situated. For instance, the space in which a surface
or surfaces are located can be assigned with directional force which will
inflect the normals of a surface, thus inflecting the shape of the surface
based on the relative position to the point from which the force is emanat-
ed. The field in which forms are defined is not neutral but can be populated by a variety of interacting forces which establish gradients of influence
in a modeling space. Gradient shapes are areas that do not have distinct
contours or edges but are instead defined by dissipation from points of
emission. These gradients are not measured based on points or coordinates
but on fields. Like a temperature map that measures the continuous and
gradual change of force across a field, these force gradients do not have
edges or contours. The spatial context within which surfaces and splines
are conceived then is also animate rather than static.

This possibility of an animate field opens up a more intricate relationship
of form and field than has been previously possible. Rather than an entity
being shaped only by its own internal definition, these topological surfaces
are inflected by the field in which they are modeled. If an entity is moved
in space, its shape might change based on the position within gradient space
even though the definition of the entity remains constant. Thus, the same
entity duplicated identically but in a different gradient space might have a
different configuration. A sequence of identical entities located in a series
through a gradient space would constitute both a self similarity and a difference based on the characteristics of the gradients and how they were
positioned. This relationship between a force and the object which stores
that force in its form is reminiscent of the insight made by Henri Bergson
in his book, *Matter and Memory*, in which he argues for a nondialectical
understanding of the relationship between substance and energy.[20] Bergson
argued that matter could not be separated from the historical process of
its becoming.

Contemporary theories of organic form, evolution, mutation and vitalism, as defined as the developmental unfolding of a structure in a gradient environment of influences, might be informative to the discussion of topology, time, and parameters as they apply to architectural design. Such discussions of organic processes often involve non-dialectical relationships between matter and information, form and time, and organization and force. This resistance to treat form, time, and motion discretely is equivalent to what might be understood as an organic tradition. The thread of "*anorganic vitalism*" that runs from Leibniz through Bergson and Gilles Deleuze could underwrite such a discussion, while replacing their natural essentialism with a revised cybernetic concept of the machine as a feedback device that creates hierarchy and organization. One of the best possible models of "*anorganic vitalism*" is the proposition of "*fused assemblages*" put forward by Lynne Margulis. The major revision to concepts of holism that Margulis introduces is from a predetermined identity to identities of becoming. Margulis formulated the evolutionary hypothesis that micro-organisms evolve their complexity by incorporating simpler organisms into larger multiplicities that become capable of reproduction as a singularity.[21] Thus, organisms are seen as previously free living colonies of organs that become a fused singularity. In her schema, there is little difference between a single body and an ecology of organisms, as both exploit one another's functions and machinic behaviors through feedback and exchange. A body, Margulis suggests, is the fused assemblage of an ecosystem operating with a high degree of continuity and stability. There is no essential structure to such an assemblage that one can uncover or deduce, at either the macro or micro scale. It is a logic of differentiation, exchange, and assemblage within an environment of gradient influences. The form, or shape, most often cited in reference to such an environment is that of the landscape. The epigenetic landscape is a theoretical and analytic device used to describe the relationship between an evolving form, or organism, within its developmental field, or environment.

Producing a geometric form from a differential equation is problematic without a differential approach to series and repetition. There are two kinds of series: a discrete, or repetitive series and a continuous, or iterative series. In a continuous or iterative series, the difference between each object in the sequence is critical and individual to each repetition. If the difference is the product of three or more variables, and if those three variables are unrelated, then the change between each iteration will be nonlinear in its structure and it will therefore be difficult to predict with absolute precision. Each step is thus dependent on the precise position of each of three or more variables; meaning that the future position

33

of the iterative series cannot be calculated outside of the series itself. In an incremental, discrete series, the differences that accompany each repetition are linear and reducible. The entire infinite set of possible futures of the series can be calculated in advance with a simple mathematical equation. In the case of the continuous series such exact definitions are impossible to determine at the beginning, as the beginning is not an origin but merely a point of departure. The future possible positions of a continuous series must be thought of as a continuum rather than as an enclosed infinity. This points to the important distinction between the infinite and the continuous, two terms which are often casually conflated. Difference and repetition, when thought of in a continuous rather than discrete manner, mandate a thinking in duration rather than in points.

This difference is crucial to an understanding of the spatial difference between the infinite and the continuous. A continuous series can be "infinitized," or reduced, through "iterative reduction," leaving a single, ideal type. In this method, a limited set of variation is organized in a series so that its continuous differences can be progressively eliminated, leaving a discrete type that can then be infinitely extended. This method of iterative reduction can be attributed to Edmund Husserl, as it is central to his invention of phenomenology.

Motion and time are similarly taken away then added back to architecture. Architectural space is infinitized by removing motion and time through iterative reduction. They are then added back typically through phenomenology. The dynamic concept of architecture, however, assumes that in any form there are inflections that direct motion and provoke and influence the forces moving through, over, under and around surfaces. The form is the site for the calculation of multiple forces. This is the case in the example of the sailboat, where on the hull's surface multiple points of sail are calculated and resolved in the form itself. The perception of the hull does not require the resolution of multiple vectors of movement as those vectors are stored in the object itself as potential energy or flow within a gradient field of forces. Moreover, the primary method of experiencing these vector effects is not optical or through aesthetic contemplation but instead through performance. The vector flows that are calculated and stored in the shape of the hull can be unfolded through both aesthetic analyses and use. Perhaps the best precedent for the unfolding of curved space is evident in the concept of Frederick Keisler's "*endlessness*" along with Adolf Loos's concept of the "*raumplan*" from which it was derived while Kiesler was working in Loos's office.[22] Although a discussion of the counter tradition of modern endless space versus the canonical modern tradition of infinite space is not possible here, the difference from the more classical and reductive models of modern form should be recognized.

The best model for the discussion of non-reducible forms of motion might be to return to the model of the landscape or the oblique ground, where motion is stored in the gradient slopes of a surface across which an object moves. Here the potential motion of an object across a surface is stored in a virtual manner as future potential energy. To return to the force discussions, the influence of a gradient space of force and energy is built into the spline networks through the inflection of their normals. A landscape is a ground that has been inflected by the historical flows of energy and movement across its surface. These historical forces manifest a geological form of development that is inflected and shaped by the flows that have moved across it. These slow transformational processes result in forms which are oriented with motion, both the virtual motion of their history and the actual motion they initiate through their slopes and valleys. This animation of slow form with the historical processes of gradual geological becoming is a paradigm of motion and time that renders substance virtually animated and actually stable. Rhythmic motion is manifest in stable-oriented form rather than in literally moving objects. In the words of Hans Jenny,

> . . . Nature reveals an abundance of sculptured forms, and all of them, it must be remembered, are the result of vibration. If the tome ceases, the mass 'freezes.' Looking at these vibrational effects, it would be no exaggeration to speak of a true magnetocymatics with its own dynamokinetic morphology. Experiments like this based on pure empiricism stimulate the plastic imagination and develop the power to feel oneself into a space permeated by forces.[23]

The work of Hans Jenny in the 1950s and 1960s is undoubtably the best example of the study of how oscillating, fluctuating, gradient fields of forces can produce not only patterns but forms. The primary theme that runs through Jenny's writings about these experiments is the continuous character between the forms produced and the fields from which they emerged. For example, Jenny argues that in the case of "the vibrational field it can be shown that every part is, in the true sense, implicated in the whole."[24] His experiments consisted of the effects of vibrations on a particulate concrete medium. The concrete forms he studied were in an environment where vibration and wave phenomenon were inherent to the system of form generation and evolution. He gave these structures the name "cymatics" meaning the "characteristic phenomenology of vibrational effects and wave phenomenon with typical structural patterns and dynamics."[25] In general, Jenny pioneered the use of viscous particle flows on plates that were both vibrating and magnetized. His techniques varied from the study of iron fillings on

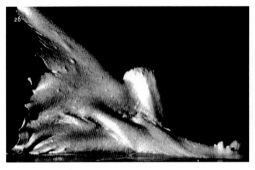
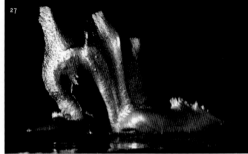

Figure 26 and 27:
A sequence of flowable mass through a vibrational magnetic field by Hans Jenny. "*These figures show the plastic pattern of movements displayed by a ferromagnetic mass in a magnetic field under the influence of vibrations. The mass flows in the magnetic space and reflects its configurations. It writhes, rears up, and stretches out but always in a way that reflects the situation in the magnetic field at that particular time,*" From Jenny, vol 2 of *Cymatics: Wave Phenomenon Vibrational Effects Harmonic Oscillations with their Structure, Kinetics and Dynamics,* (Basel: Basilius Press, 1974), 62.

Figures 28 and 29:
Jenny's description of the formation of these forms in magnetic space takes the language of architectural struc-
ture as he mentions both arches and walls.
"*Under other conditions there are upfoldings which rise up to form arches. These structures tower up and tend to flow along a path. Then they thrust out again into space, and in the interplay between the cohesion of the mass and the mag-netic force they spread, grow thin, and peter out. Forms tower up displaying the configuration wrought by magnetic force and oscillation. Large leaflike walls take shape and sway to and fro in the magnetic field.*" Jenny, *Cymatics,* 61.

plates to the sandwiching of fluids between vibrating glass plates. Jenny also used motion pictures to capture the movement of these forms within the magnetic pathways of oscillating fields. His method was to study the motion sequences of the forms rather than their static form. Previously, particles of filings and other materials were treated as discrete elements that would form a pattern that was coincident with the geometry of the plate. By introducing viscosity to the particles thus forming a continuous semi-solid flow, Jenny was able to study the shaping of form in free space rather than in two-dimensional pattern only. By varying the Reynolds numbers of these particles suspended in a fluid, he was able to develop an intuition into the morphology of forms within magnetic fields. His studies involved the famil-iar use of a vibrating plate that would configure iron filings into patterns. Added to this influence was the presence of magnetic fields to impose polar patterns on the filings. These forces were then thought of in terms of peri-odic excitement by both the vibration oscillation and the changing position of the magnet. Thus the forms that emerged were studied both in their form and in the ways in which they would follow the magnetic pathways. The play between two types of fields, magnetic and vibrational, produced form. The character of these forms were persistence and continuity, but, unlike discrete reducible forms, they remained continuous with the fields within which they were generated. Rather than making shapes through the familiar operations of a sculptor or architect, through direct manipulation

28

29

Figures 30 and 31:
"*These masses have solidified under vibration. The relief is complicated in structure because each of the various stages of consistency the mass has passed through while solidifying has left its imprint. There are large billow-like formations and tiny wrinkles, wave trains succeeding one another, and sudden changes in the direction of flow. It is as if the 'history' of the process had been recorded in transverse and longitudinal folds. There is also a tendency for a latticework of folds to take shape.*" Jenny, Cymatics, 63.

Figures 32 and 33 (next page): "*A flowable mass assumes a characteristic pattern under the influence of a high-frequency tone. Trains of waves take shape. The substance forms into a lump which, because adhesion is reduced, glides round in one piece. The substance forms bays and promontories, spreads out thinly and is then thrown into folds which make a rugged relief.*" Jenny, Cymatics, 18–19.

30

31

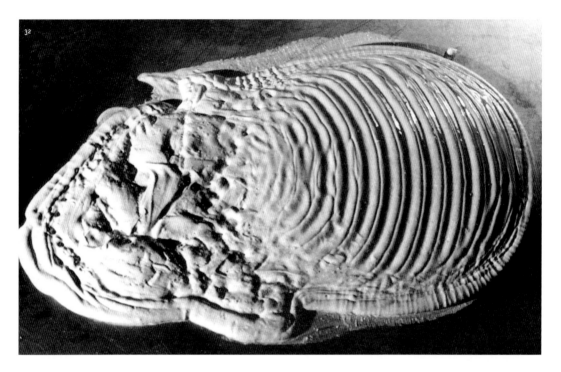

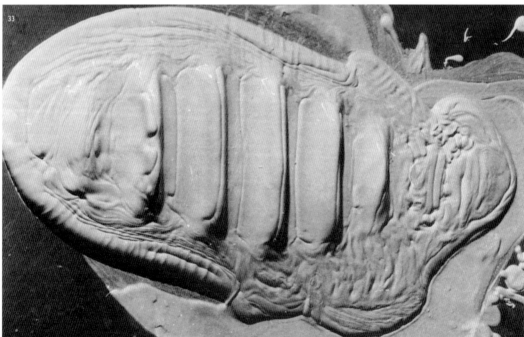

of material for example, Jenny modulated form through oscillating frequencies and parameters. Jenny sculpted form through the adjustment of oscillators without forfeiting his intuition to a machine intelligence. The shift from sculptural techniques of whittling, carving, chipping, and scraping material to the modulation, oscillation, and vibration of particles does not mandate the relinquishment of creativity to machinery. Instead, it suggests the creative manipulation of a flow of parameters in time.

The use of parameters and statistics for the design of form requires a more abstract, and often less representational origin for design. The shape of statistics, or parameters, may yield a culturally symbolic form, yet at the beginning, their role is more inchoate. A return to the discussion of the orrery might supply two terms: the "concrete assemblage" and the "abstract machine." For example, in Étienne-Louis Boullée's Cenotaph to Newton, the orrery operates as both an abstract model and as a sign. The orrery, in the sense that it represents the movements and organization of a centered and harmonically regulated universe, is a concrete assemblage. To the degree that it is a diagram for centralized harmonic regulation, like a compass, it is an abstract machine. The diagram for the orrery can be seen to circulate among many institutional and symbolic regimes where it takes on many meanings. As a statement of centralized regulation, however, its abstract performance is consistent. Any abstract machine, such as an orrery, can be understood as both a technical statement and as a signifier. Neither its representational nor its technical structure can be understood independently. The difference between its abstract and representational roles can be located precisely at the moment it crosses the technological threshold from being a diagram to a concrete assemblage. The use of the term abstraction here is not intended to be confused with the purist or modern notion of visual abstraction. In those instances abstraction involves an aesthetic reduction to fixed formal essences through the paring away of differences. An alternative concept of abstraction, one that is more generative and evolutionary, involves proliferation, expansion and unfolding. This marks a shift from a modernist notion of abstraction based on form and vision to an abstraction based on process and movement. In order to define such a diagrammatic regime, it is perhaps most helpful to cite Michel Foucault's terms; "abstract machine" and "diagram." Gilles Deleuze has referred to these terms as "asignifying concepts." By definition, an asignifying concept is instrumental before it is representational. This model depends on the precise distinction between "linguistic constructions" and "statements." Linguistic constructions, such as propositions or phrases, can always be attributed to particular referents. Statements, on the other hand, are not initially linguistic but are machinic processes.[26] For instance, the sequence of letters **Q, W, E, R, T, Y** is distributed on a typewriter or computer keyboard to produce words. The logic of their sequential distribution is based on the control of the speed at which one can potentially type words in the English language. There is no single sentence or word that tests this distribution but rather an indefinite series of existing and future words. Because there is an open series the system must be characterized as indefinitely structured. The keyboard is an actual machine, or concrete assemblage, because it is technological. But the distribution of its letters on keys in space is a virtual diagram, or an abstract machine. Statements such as these are machinic techniques, discursive concepts, or schemata that precede the representational and linguistic effects they facilitate. Signifiers are not rejected but delayed toward the moment that they are "*found at the intersection of different systems and are cut across by the statement acting in the role of primitive function.*"[27] Linguistic constructions are merely postponed, not abolished, and a regime of abstract, schematic statements are seen to preempt and sponsor them. From the particular discursive formation of multiple, diagonally intersecting statements, some form of expression emerges. Through the interaction of a multiplicity of abstract statements, signifiers emerge in a more dynamic manner than mere representational effects might. The shift from linguistic models to the proliferation of asignifying statements marks what Deleuze terms a move from the "*archive*" to the "*diagram.*"[28] The move from linguistic constructions to statements, or more properly from meaning to machine, is a necessary shift in sensibility if one is to tap the potential of abstract machines such as computational motion geometry and time-based, dynamic force simulations.

This shift is the primary explanation for the apparent alliance between certain aspects of Deleuze and Foucault's discourse and many contemporary architects now weary of representational critiques spanning from stylistic postmodernism to deconstruction. In Deleuze's interpretation of Foucault's critique of panopticism, concrete architectural form is transformed into abstract machinic instrumentality. Techniques, as opposed to technology, become an expression of cultural, social, and political relations rather than as an essential power. The effects of abstract machines trigger the formation of concrete assemblages when their virtual diagrammatic relationships are actualized as a technical possibility. Concrete assemblages are realized only when a new diagram can make them cross the technical threshold. It is the already social diagrams that select the new technologies. It is in the spirit of the abstract technical statement yet to become concrete that topologies, animation and parameter-based modeling are being explored here. In order to bring these technologies into a discipline that is defined as the site of translation from the virtual into the concrete, it is necessary that we first interrogate their abstract structure. Without a detailed understanding of their performance as diagrams and organizational techniques it is impossible to begin a discussion of their translation into architectural form. The availability and rapid colonization of architectural design by computer-aided techniques presents the discipline with yet another opportunity to both retool and rethink itself as it did with the advent of stereometric projection and perspective. If there is a single concept that must be engaged due to the proliferation of topological shapes and computer-aided tools, it is that in their structure as abstract machines, these technologies are animate.

Endnotes:

1. For varied and rigorous discussions of the animal as the surrogate, model and metaphor for architecture in history, theory and design see the chapter "Donkey Urbanism" in Catherine Ingraham's book *Architecture and the Burdens of Linearity* (New Haven: Yale University Press, 1998) as well as her essay "Animals 2: The Problem of Distinction (Insects, For Example)" in *Assemblage* 14 (Cambridge, 1991), 25-29.

2. It is important to any discussion of parameter-based design that there be both the unfolding of an internal system and the infolding of contextual information fields. This issue of contextualism is discussed more extensively in my essay "Architectural Curvilinearity: The Folded, the Pliant and the Supple," in *Architectural Design* 102, *Folding in Architecture* (London, 1993) where in the same volume it is also criticized by Jeffrey Kipnis in his essay "Towards a New Architecture."

3. There are two instances of architectural theorists and designers crossing over from models of cinema to models of animation. The first is Brian Boigon's "*The Cartoon Regulators*" in *Assemblage*, 19 (Cambridge, 1992), 66-71. The second is Mark Rakatansky's discussions of the writing and animation of Chuck Jones regarding theories of mobility, action, and gesture in *Any Magazine* 23 (New York, 1998).

4. Siegfried Giedion, *Mechanization Takes Command: A Contribution to Anonymous History* (New York: Oxford University Press, 1948). See also Giedion's *Space, Time and Architecture* (Cambridge: Harvard University Press, 1967).

5. See Sanford Kwinter's "Landscapes of Change" in *Assemblage* 19 (Cambridge, 1992), 50-65.

6. Colin Rowe and Robert Slutsky, "Transparency: Literal and Phenomenal," in *The Mathematics of the Ideal Villa and Other Essays* (Cambridge: MIT Press, c1976).

7. Kenneth Frampton, in "Frontality vs. Rotation" in *Five Architects: Eisenman, Graves, Gwathmey, Hejduk, Meier* (New York: Oxford University Press, 1975), 9-13.

8. The trace has been defined primarily by Jacques Derrida, Peter Eisenman and Bernard Tschumi. Both Bernard Tschumi and Peter Eisenman have referred to the concept of the trace as the representation of time-based processes through simultaneity and seriality. Tschumi captured movement as still frames from a story board in the cinematically inspired *The Manhattan Transcripts* (London: Academy Additions, 1981). Peter Eisenman has worked with traces for the notation of multiple archeological moments and steps in a design process throughout his career. The first method of tracing in Eisenman's work appeared in both his early houses and later in the Aronoff Center at the University of Cincinatti. Harry Cobb has argued that these traces of transformational processes constitute a new form of architectural ornament in the book *Eleven Authors in Search of a Building: The Aronoff Center for Design and Art at the University of Cincinnati*, ed. Cynthia Davidson (New York: Monacelli Press, 1996).

9. Andrew Benjamin's discussion of "*timing*" discriminates between two models of complexity; the first, associated with Descartes, is one of a complex order made of simpler orders; the other, associated with Leibniz, is a complexity of ensembles whose individual and collective order exists "*at the same time.*" "*Here the ensemble in question involves the belonging together of that which resists synthetic unity. The existence of the monad as an already existent ensemble means that the monad is an original ensemble, i.e. an ensemble in which differential plurality is not a consequence of the event, on the contrary it is constitutive of the event—the relational ensemble—itself.*" Andrew Benjamin, *The Plural Event: Descartes, Hegel, Heidegger* (London: Routledge, 1993), 125.

10. Motion and time have been understood as "*vague essences*" because they could not be dimensioned within a static system of point description. The term "*vague essences*" is meant to indicate the properties of forces, behaviors, and relationships that are inherently dynamic and indeterminate and that can not be reduced and quantified once and for all. As Lucia Irigaray has argued, because of a persistent Cartesianism, there has been a historic inattention to these temporally and formally indeterminate systems of organization and sciences of vague essences. See the chapter "The Mechanics of Fluids" in Luce Irigaray's book *This Sex Which Is Not One*, trans. Catherine Porter (Ithaca: Cornell University Press, 1985), 106-118.

11. A rare insidence of a philosophical, technical, and historical treatment of topology and calculus in regard to architectural design is Bernard Cache, *Earth Moves: The Furnishing of Territories*, trans. Anne Boyman, ed. Michael Speaks (Cambridge: MIT Press, 1995).

12. This comment is made in reference to a short text co-written by the editors of *Assemblage* comparing Buckminster Fuller's use of "geodesics" with Jesse Reiser's use of "geodetics," based on the sim-

larity of triangulated surfaces in *Assemblage* 26 (Cambridge, 1997).

13. See Gilles Deleuze's discussion of Henri Bergson in the chapter "Intuition as Method" in his book *Bergsonism*, trans. Hugh Tomlinson and Barbara Habberjam (New York: Zone Books, 1991).

14. In conversation, Rob Shaw explained that the thousands of hours spent in front of a computer screen watching visualizations of chaotic equations was a method of training oneself to recognize those same behaviors intuitively. Rob Shaw and Doyne Farmer were the first people to map the non-periodic behavior in a dripping faucet.

15. A catenoid is a curve defined as a hanging weighted string. Catenoidal curves have been used previously by Antoni Gaudí, Frei Otto and other structural expressionists.

16. See my book *Folds, Bodies and Blobs: Collected Essays* (Brussels: La Lettre Volée, 1998).

17. Thompson, D'Arcy. On Growth and Form (Cambridge: Cambridge University Press, 1961).

18. Francois Dagognet, *Étienne-Jules Marey: A Passion for the Trace* (New York: Zone Books, 1992), 62.

19. Pamela Johnston, ed. AA Documents 3: The function of the oblique, The architecture of Claude Parent and Paul Virilio 1963-1969 (London: Architectural Association Publications, 1996).

20. See Henri Bergson, *Matter and Memory*, trans. Nancy Margaret Paul and W. Scott Palmer (New York: Zone Books, 1988) and also Bergson, *Creative Evolution*, trans. Arthur Mitchell, with a foreword by Irwin Edman (New York: The Modern Library, 1944).

21. LynneMargulis, and Dorian Sagan, *Microcosmos: Four Billion Years of Evolution from Our Microbial Ancestors* (Berkeley: University of California Press, 1997).

22. For a discussion of the tradition of "*endlessness*" initiated by Keisler see "Dieter Bogner, Bart Lootsma, Greg Lynn, Lars Spuybroek" in *Cahier* 6 (Rotterdam, 1997), 93-104.

23. Hans Jenny, *Cymatics: Wave Phenomena, Vibrational Effects, Harmonic Oscillations with their Structure, Kinetics and Dynamics*, vol. 2 (Basel: Basilius Press, 1974), 58.

24. Jenny, *Cymatics*, 9.

25. Jenny, *Cymatics*, 7.

26. "*Foucault gives it its most precise name: it is a 'diagram', that is to say a 'functioning, abstracted from any obstacle [. . .] or friction [and which] must be detached from any specific use. The diagram is no longer an auditory visual archive but a map, a cartography that is coextensive with the whole social field. It is an abstract machine.*" Gilles Deleuze, *Foucault*, trans. Seán Hand, foreword by Paul Bové (Minneapolis: University of Minnesota, 1988), 34.

27. Deleuze, Ibid, 39.

28. This argument has been developed more extensively in reference to the work of Ben Van Berkel and his office's use of diagramming as a strategy for beginning the design process in "Forms of Expression: The Proto-Functional Potential of Diagrams in Architectural Design" in *El Croquis* 72/73 (Madrid, 1995).

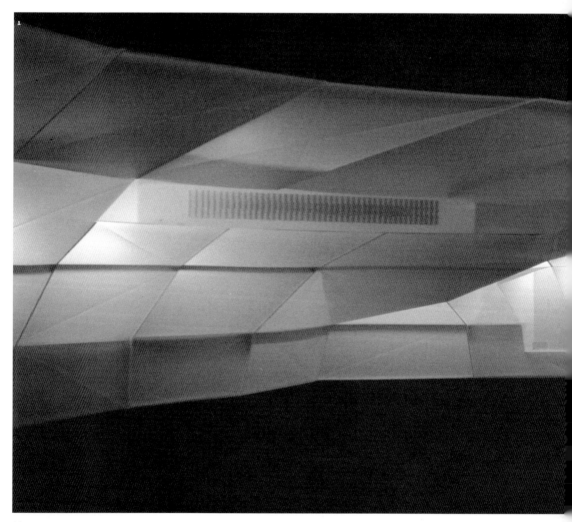

artists space
new york city

The installation of four projects at Artists Space was treated as a full-scale exhibit in itself. Thus, the installation reflected both the spatial character of the gallery and the design processes of the four projects exhibited. The complex forms of the exhibition were realized through two-dimensional plots from computer files. The resulting templates were cut from vinyl and plastic panels, which were then assembled in the exhibition space and hung on the walls. They were covered by a pleated mylar skin, thus creating a continuous surface.

Figure 1 (previous page):
View of the installation.

Figure 2:
View of the entry to the installation looking through the opening cut into the existing gallery wall.

Figure 3:
View toward the Cardiff Opera House node.

Figure 4:
View toward the Port Authority node.

Figure 5:
View looking between the Port Authority and Yokohama Port Terminal nodes.

Figure 6:
View toward the Yokohama Port Terminal node.

Figure 7:
View toward the Long Island House Prototype node.

Figure 8:
Enlarged view of the Cardiff Opera House node.

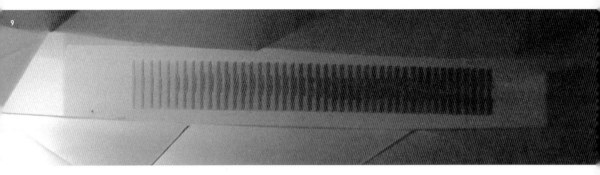

Figure 9:
Model of the structural fins of the Yokohama Port Terminal, laser-cut from translucent orange acrylic sheets.

Figure 10:
Eight stereolithography models of the Yokohama Port Terminal showing both the individual programmatic tubes and the composite tubular massing of the project. On the right is a model of the structural fins, identical to the model in Figure 9, but cut at 1/6th the size.

Figure 11 (opposite):
View of the Yokohama Port Terminal node of the installation.

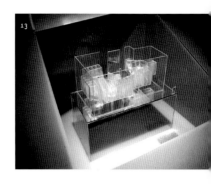

Figure 12:
View of the entry to the installation, showing the Artists Space
Installation node. This node contains a model of the gallery space
and installation.

Figure 13:
Miniature stereolithography model of the gallery space and
installation.

Figure 14:
Construction view of the entry to the installation.

Figure 15:
Various stereolithography models of the House Prototype in
Long Island.

Figure 16:
A series of stereolithography models of the House Prototype
showing rapid prototypes of a 240-frame animation sequence
every 30 frames. The larger models are rapid prototypes of the
180th and 240th frames of the animation.

Figure 17 (opposite):
View of the House Prototype in Long Island node.

17

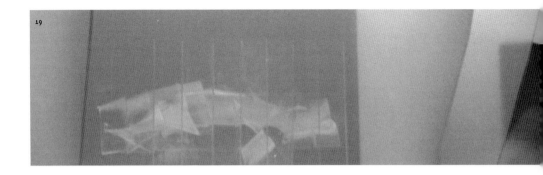

Figure 18:
View of the Port Authority node.

Figure 19:
Stereolithography and laser-cut acrylic model of the Port Authority project.

Figure 20:
Stereolithography model of one bay of the Port Authority project.

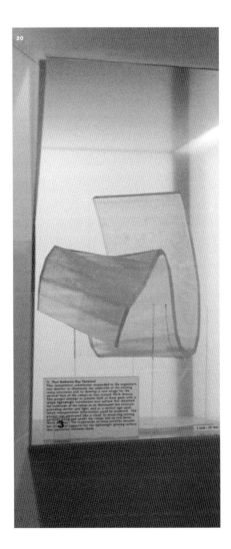

Figure 21:
Cardiff Bay Opera House models.

Figure 22:
View of the Cardiff Bay Opera House node of the installation.

Figure 23 (opposite):
At right, stereolithography model of the Opera House Hall
mounted on a mirror. At left, stereolithography model of the
entire project, with a magnifying lens for detailed viewing by the
visitors.

23

Figures 24–27:
Views of the installation space during construction, before apply-
ing the mylar surface.

Figures 28 and 30:
Views of installation during construction. The hand cut "Sintra"
vinyl fins and support bracing are both glued and screwed
together, making a lightweight frame to which the facetted mylar
surface has been applied with double-sided tape.

Figure 29:
Construction view of installation from above.

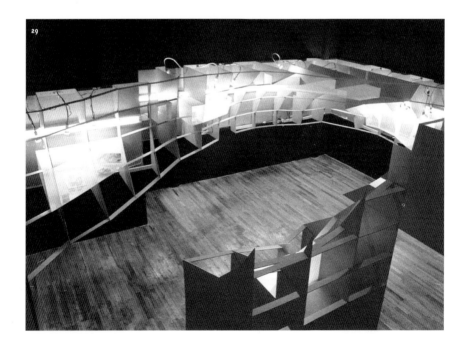

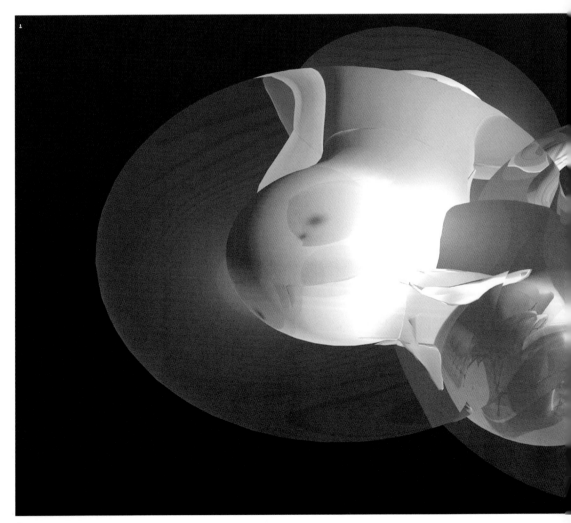

Artists space
Installation Design

The exhibit at Artists Space presented a process of design for five projects, emphasizing virtual conception over actual end-product. Thus, the exhibit and the elements in it were presented in both virtual and actual forms. The virtual designs were displayed at a micro-scale within a space that exhibited the qualities and characteristics of the spaces presented in miniature. The installation in the gallery space itself was an actualization in various plastic materials of this virtual exhibit. Computer-generated animations accompanied miniature built models of selected stages of the animation sequences. These complex organic forms were constructed through three-dimensional plots from computer files, using rapid prototyping and three-dimensional printing techniques such as laser-cut metal plates and stereolithography. These models are extremely small (less than ten square feet), yet maintain a high degree of detail, within a micron. The exhibition was also available in digital format on the internet magazine *Basilisk*. It could be visited as either a rendered animation sequence, as an interactive series of rendered still images, or as a downloadable, texture-mapped, three-dimensional file.

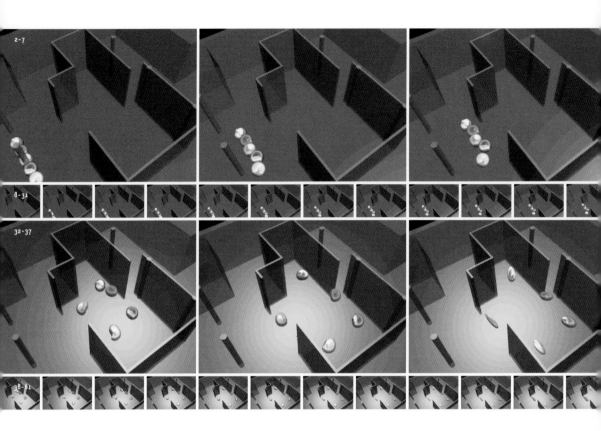

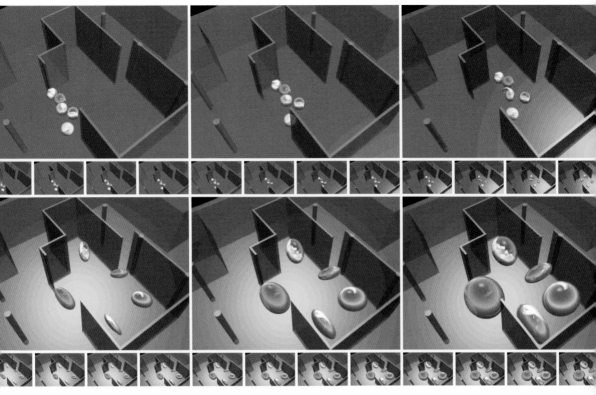

Figure 1: (previous page)
The original envelope from which the Artists Space Gallery Installation was constructed. Each of the four projects, plus the exhibition design, was located in the gallery space with an individual node. Each of these nodes was defined with a sphere of influence that affected the other four nodes. Through the interaction of these zones of influence the five project nodes fused into a single continuous surface. The particular patterns on each of the objects result from the fact that each of the five project nodes is rendered with an image of the project which it contains.

Figures 2 - 31:
The five individual project nodes located in reference to the existing gallery space. Each of the four projects was located at a corner location where the existing walls intersected, with the exhibition design node located at the entry to the gallery space. The five project nodes were organized in a chronological sequence moving clockwise around the projects space.

Figures 32 - 61:
Once located, the sphere of influence of each project was expanded to fill the local surroundings of its gallery space. Within the zone of influence, each node was given an equal force of attraction on the other four nodes. Based on these influences they were later connected into a continuous surface or "blob."

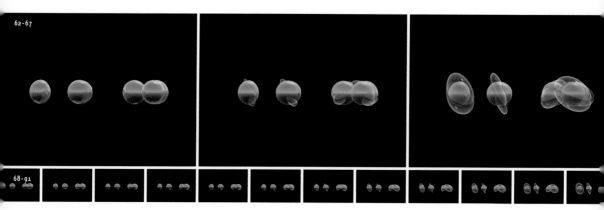

Figures 62-91:
Development of the alignment and orientation of the five individual elements in reference to one another. These alignments are based on the position of the project nodes in the locations of the gallery space.

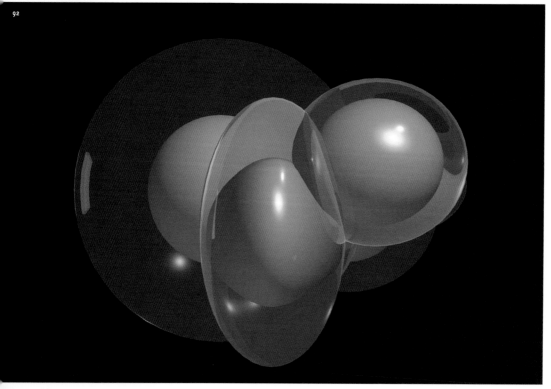

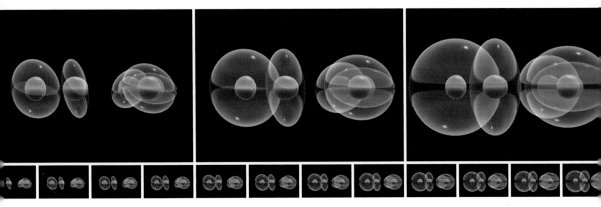

Figure 92 (opposite):
Elevation of the resulting organization of the five project nodes with their respective zones of influence.

Figure 93:
Axonometric of the five project nodes with their respective zones of influence.

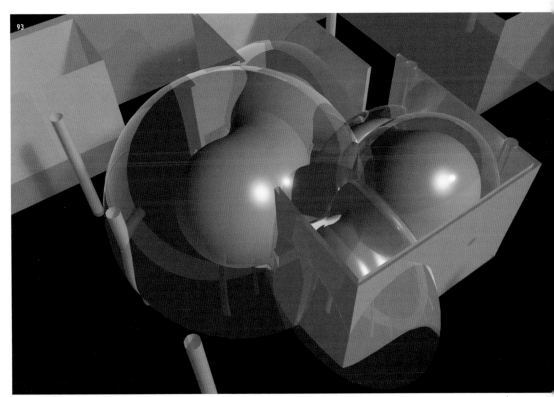

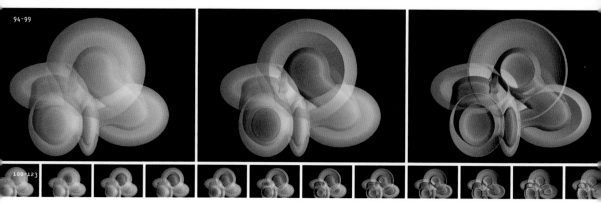

Figures 94-123:
A sequence of sections through the blob structure that was generated by fusing the five independent nodes together into a single, continuous surface. This surface retains the original primitives as well as the original zones of influence that determined the degree of connection between specific nodes.

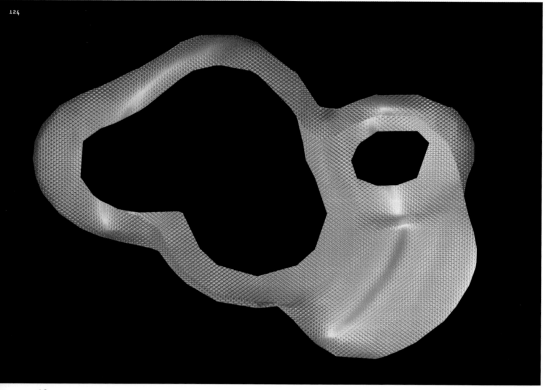

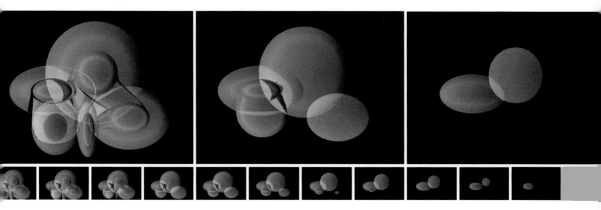

Figure 124 (opposite):
From the entire enclosed surface, two sections were removed: everything from the floor to three feet above floor level, and everything seven feet above floor level. This is the remaining surface, as seen from above.

Figure 125:
Transverse elevation view of the remaining surface.

Figure 126:
Longitudinal elevation view of the remaining surface.

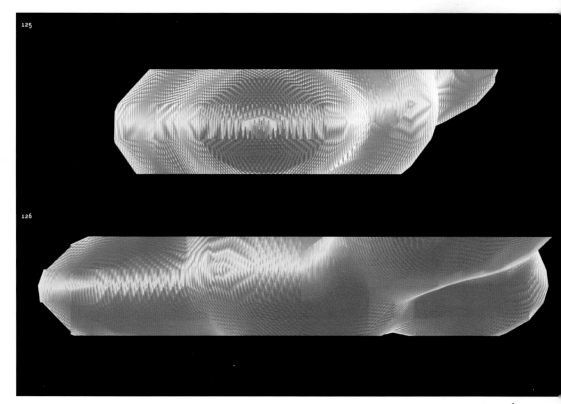

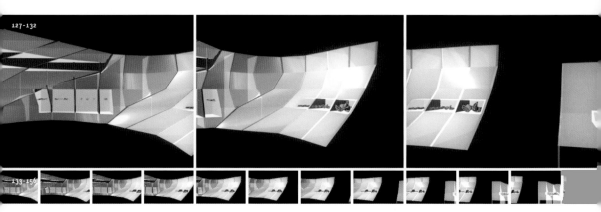

Figures 127-156:
Clockwise sequence of views of the installation, taken from the center of the gallery space.

Figure 157:
View from above the installation space showing the mylar surface, the translucent vitrines, and the support fins that attach to the existing walls.

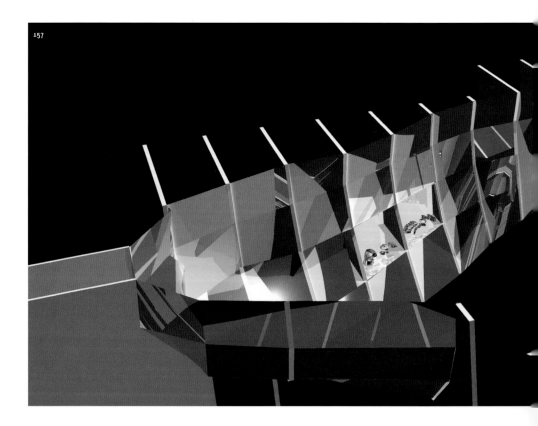

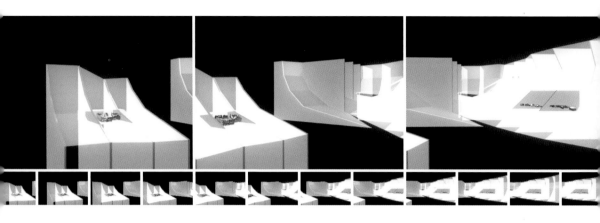

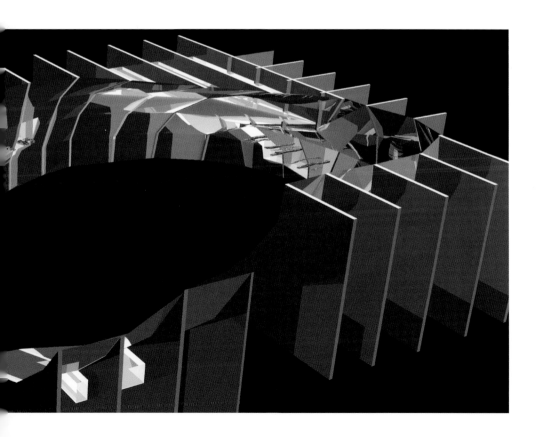

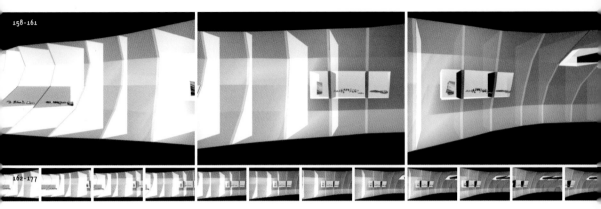

Figures 158-177:
Continuation of the clockwise sequence that began with the previous images 127-156 (previous page).

Figure 178:
View from within the installation space. The entry is at right.

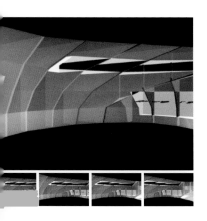

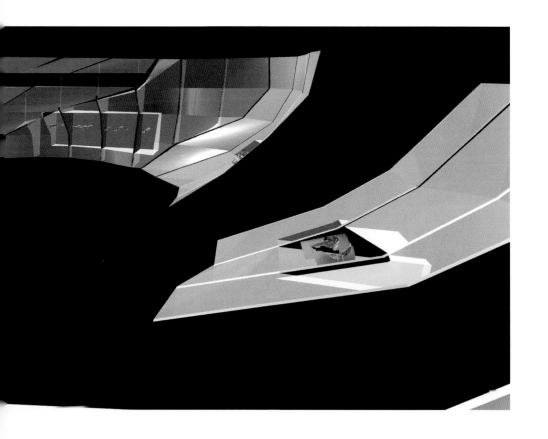

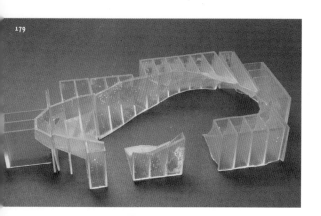

Figure 179–181:
The stereolithography model of the exhibition space interior. Approximate size 6" x 8".

199

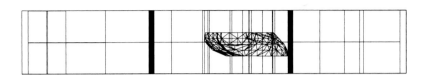

201

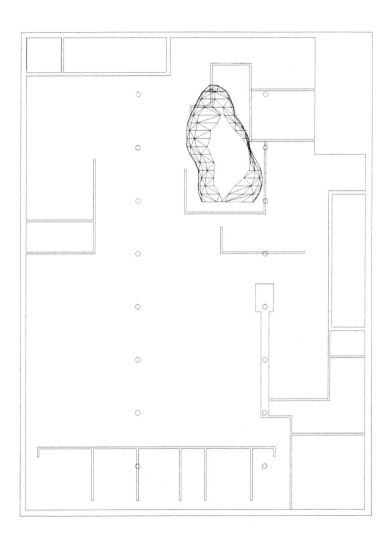

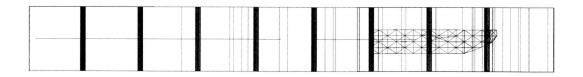

202

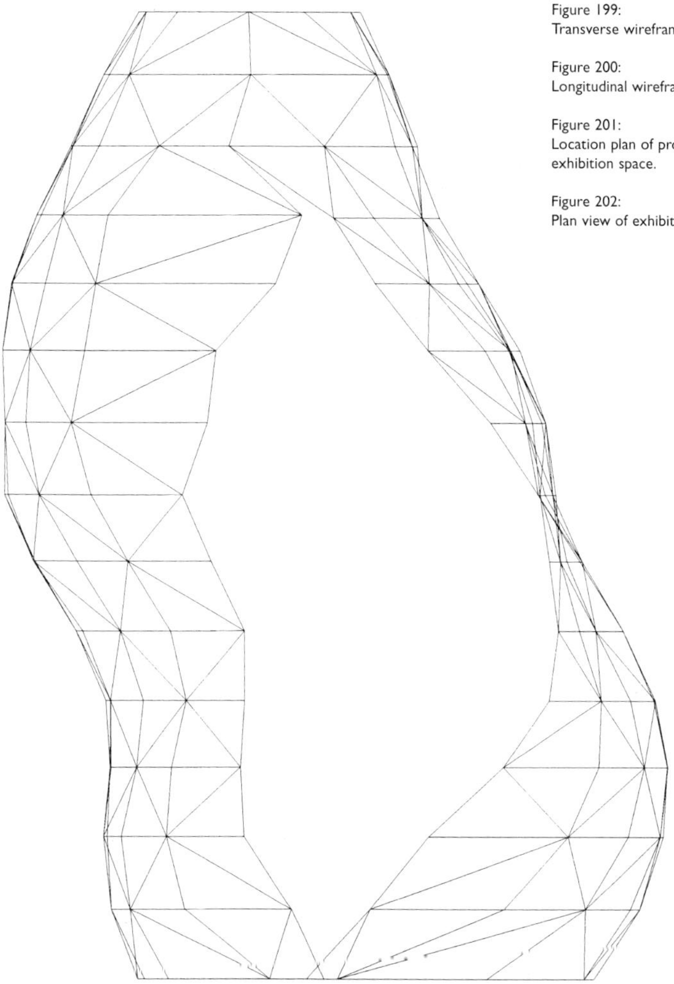

Figure 199:
Transverse wireframe elevation.

Figure 200:
Longitudinal wireframe elevation.

Figure 201:
Location plan of projects gallery in the entire exhibition space.

Figure 202:
Plan view of exhibition surface.

203-208

209-214

215-220

Figures 203-220:
Sections through the fin support structure.

221

222

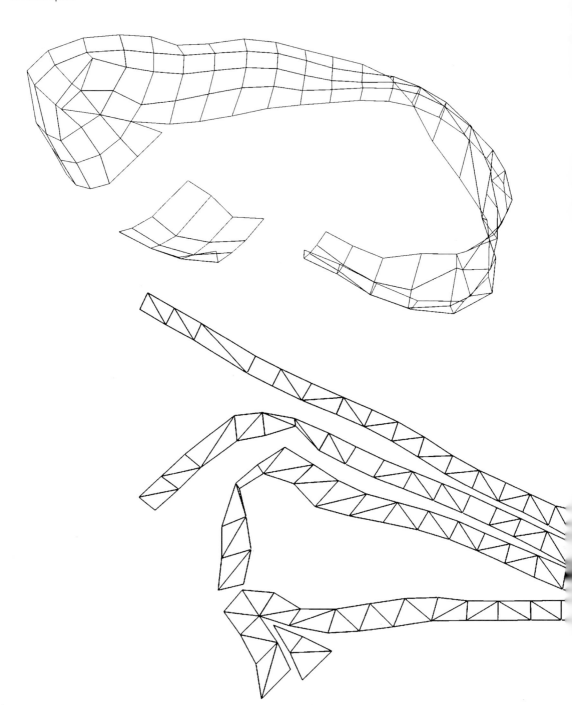

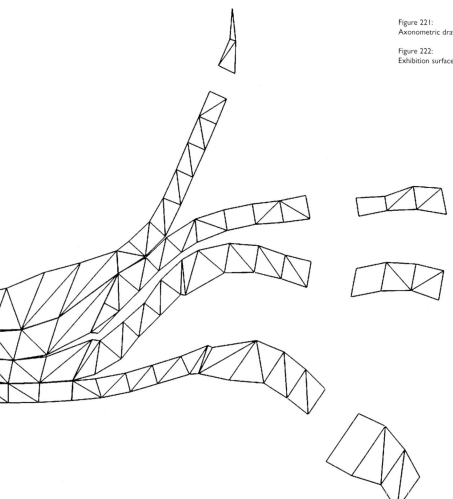

Figure 221:
Axonometric drawing of the exhibition surface.

Figure 222:
Exhibition surface unfolded into a single plane.

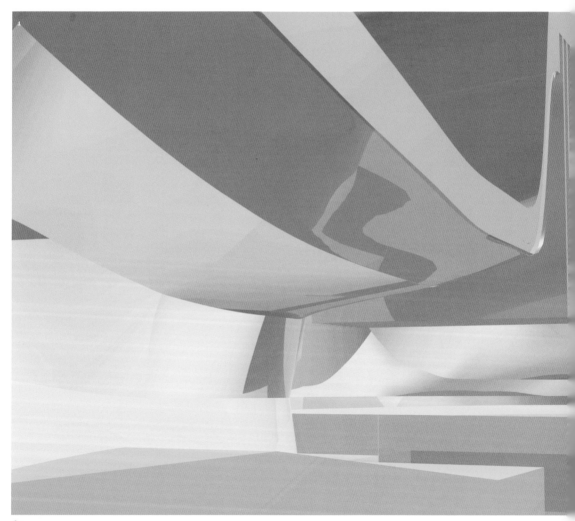

cardiff Bay opera House competition

The siting of the Welsh National Opera House on the now-defunct industrial waterfront of the Inner Harbor of Cardiff Bay mandates a new concept for waterfront urban space that is continuous with the history of the site and Cardiff's waterfront. The proposed project utilizes the empty shell of the defunct technology of the Oval Basin, not as a monument to a bygone era but as the generator of a new waterfront civic institution that is an interface between land and water. The Oval Basin is the chrysalis out of which the Opera House emerges. Cardiff's coastline is a complex edge at several scales, generating urban growth and development. By borrowing the pattern of the graving docks which slope the land into the sea, the Opera House is connected to the water through the invention of a new public reservoir space that flows under and through the site. The sunken reservoir space allows for a multipli ade. In this way, the project has not only a public space in plan surrounding the Oval Piazza, but also deploys a sectional public space. It is a civic institution that is not monolithic but permeated with public space and programs. Like the graving docks that floated the volumes of the hulls on cradle supports, the Opera House programs are housed in volumes that are supported above the reservoir. The project is structured through two systems: portalized wall fins and rib structured hulls. These two systems are sheathed in a lightweight tensile membrane that provides a sheltered but environmentally permeable space over the buildable site area. This image of the project—of a glowing alien presence within the chrysalis of a dead technological waterfront monument—allows the project to participate in the history of the site and the industrial heritage of the waterfront, while at the same time proposing a new civic institution that is continuous with the history of the site and the waterfront of the city.

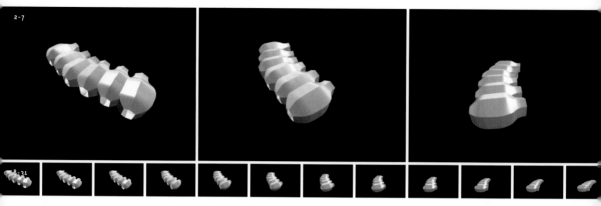

Figures 2-31:
Rendering of the rehearsal space volumes. These spaces can be subdivided into six discrete spaces or they may be a single continuous space.

Figure 38 (opposite):
Roof plan with Oval Basin.

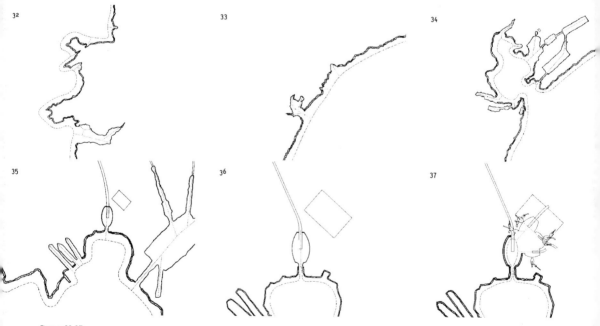

Figures 32-37:
Coastline studies. Because the site is adjacent to the Oval Basin, the waterfront's history of boat building and repair suggested that this edge be a critical feature of the project. The coastline was analyzed at various scales for self-similarity and repetition. At numerous scales, a pattern of gastrulations was discovered where the water's edge is captured by the land as rivers, bays, and harbors. These cascading shifts in scale include the Atlantic Ocean, Cardiff Bay, the inner harbor, the graving berths, and the Oval Basin.

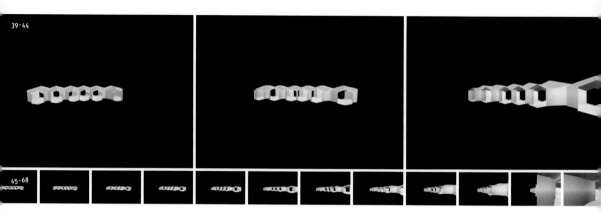

Figures 39-68:
Continuation of renderings of rehearsal space volumes.

Figure 69:
Aerial perspective of portalized fin wall structure.

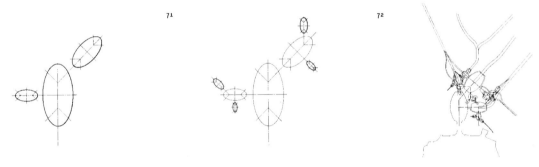

71

72

Figure 70:
One generation of oval branching. The site's proximity to the northeastern edge of the Oval Basin allows the water's edge to be brought into the site through the differential repetition of the Oval Basin. The generative diagram for the proliferation of ovals is a two-thirds-scale oval, aligned on center with the given site area. A secondary branch is located perpendicularly at one-third scale.

Figure 71:
A second generation of oval branching, following the same rules of decreasing scale and mirror symmetry.

Figures 72:
This autonomous system of branching was deployed on the site and modified by general information from the context. Ovals were stretched, turned, and aligned to connect with adjacent streets, building edges, and views. Once aligned, each connection was frozen in terms of future branching. The perimeter of this figure becomes a new waterline, where the surface of the site is flooded by a swamplike waterfront space.

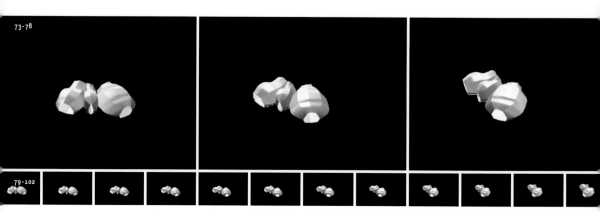

Figures 73-102:
Rendering of side stages and stage support spaces.

Figure 103:
Aerial perspective of tensile roof.

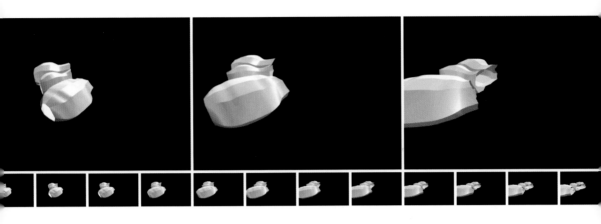

Figure 104:
The structural fins aligned along four intersecting striation patterns on ten-meter intervals. The walls follow an alignment until intersecting, at which point they branch. On crossing an alignment parallel to a previous orientation, a secondary branch is generated.

Figure 105:
Structural system of portalized fin walls, developed using the alternating branching diagram of the four striation alignments on the site.

Figure 106:
A structure of fin walls used to support the Opera House volumes above the sunken area of the site. This "swamp" edge is raked with perpendicular lines that follow several existing site alignments, including the light rail line, the building edge of the Oval Basin, the existing edge of buildings, and the highway underpass.

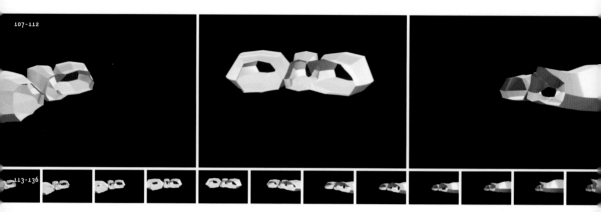

Figures 107-136:
Continuation of rendering of side stages and stage support spaces.

Figure 140 (opposite):
Aerial perspective of project.

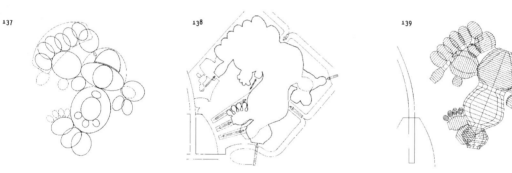

Figure 137:
The realignment and deformation of the initial programmatic volumes, based on the functional adjacencies of the foyers, opera house, stages, shops, loading, dressing rooms, and rehearsal rooms.

Figure 138:
Final configuration of the programmatic volumes in plan.

Figure 139:
The oval contours were rotated into ovoid volumes and subdivied into four-, six-, eight-, and twelve-sided volumes, depending on their relative size.

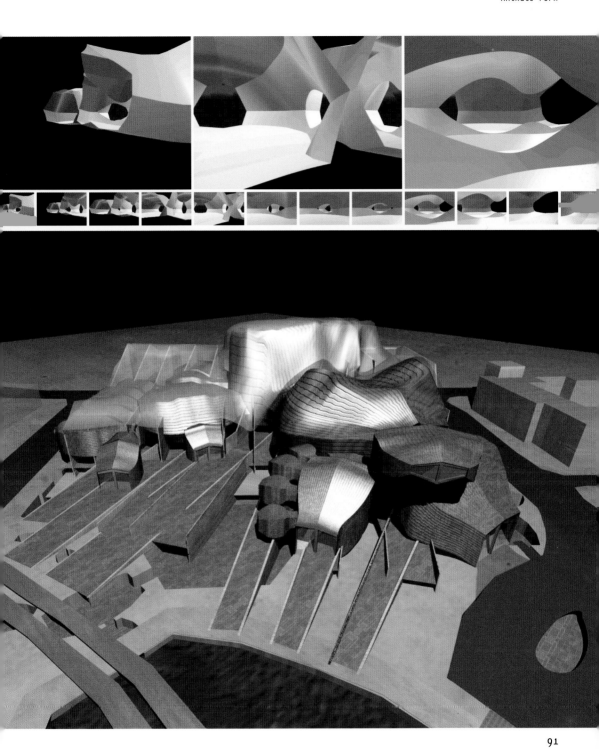

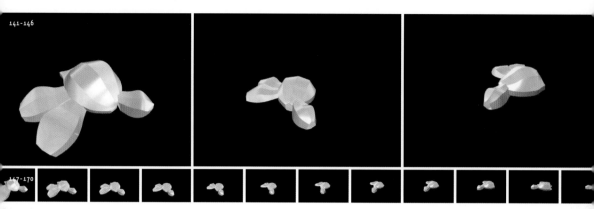

Figures 141-170:
Rendering of the audio visual control booths, recording studios, the secondary lobby, and the rear public entrance.

Figure 174 (opposite):
Aerial perspective of project from the docklands.

Figure 171:
Four polyp types: four-sided, six-sided, eight-sided, and twelve-sided. The complexity of the faceting of the volumes is related to their surface area. The smaller volumes are four-sided and simpler than the largest volumes that are twelve-sided and remain relatively smooth and deform more uniformly.

Figure 172:
Surface: the volumes are enclosed with a continuous surface that is faceted in one direction and open at both ends. The skin is constructed of metal panels similar to steel ship-building techniques.

Figure 173:
Structure: like a ship's hull, the volumes are structured on their surface with transfer beams and ridge beams that extend along their length. The ridge beams are supported by columns on-center at each end of the volume. The transfer beams allow the volumes to be supported at arbitrary alignments to the portalized walls which support them.

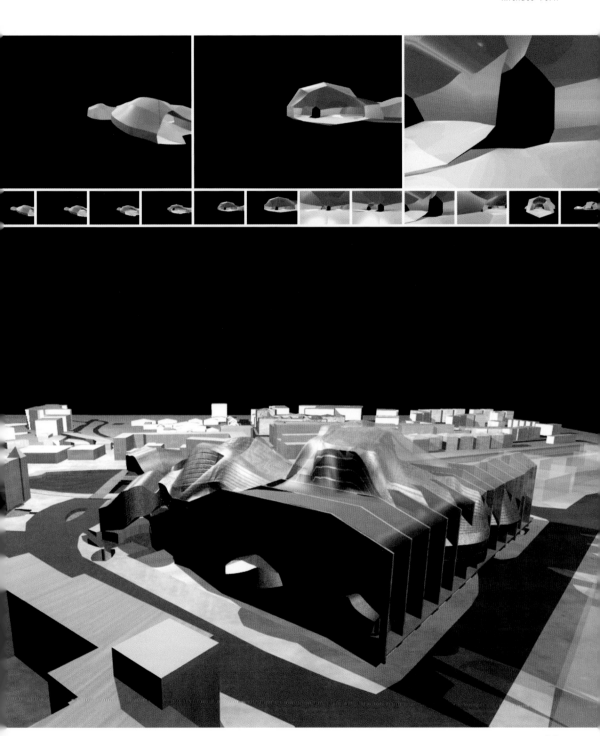

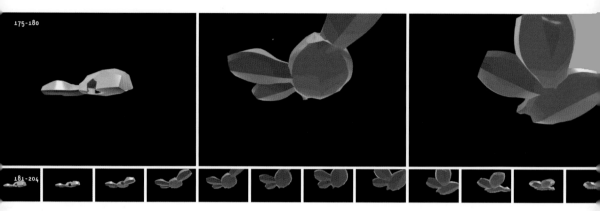

Figures 175-204:
Continuation of rendering of audio visual control booths, recording studios, the secondary lobby, and the rear public entrance.

Figure 208 (opposite):
Eastern elevation of project from the highway approach.

Figures 205–207:
Due to the formal affinity that was developing between the polyp-like volumes of the design and the steel-hulled boats which historically occupied the site, the 'graving dock' became the analogy for the relationship of the building to the ground. This section diagram exploits this history both urbanistically and structurally. The Opera House interior is contained in the oval volumes that are analogous to the hull, which is supported by a provisional "cradle"-like structure. This entire system is partially sunken into the site where the three-hundred-car parking garage is located half in and half out of the ground. The Opera House volumes are approached by a series of ramps. The ground plane slopes down into the sunken parking area. The steel-clad volumes are the only environmentally closed spaces in the project, yet the buildable site area as defined by the brief is covered by a translucent tensile membrane that would protect the spaces between structural fins from rain and snow. This membrane would also diffuse direct sunlight during the day and glow in the evening.

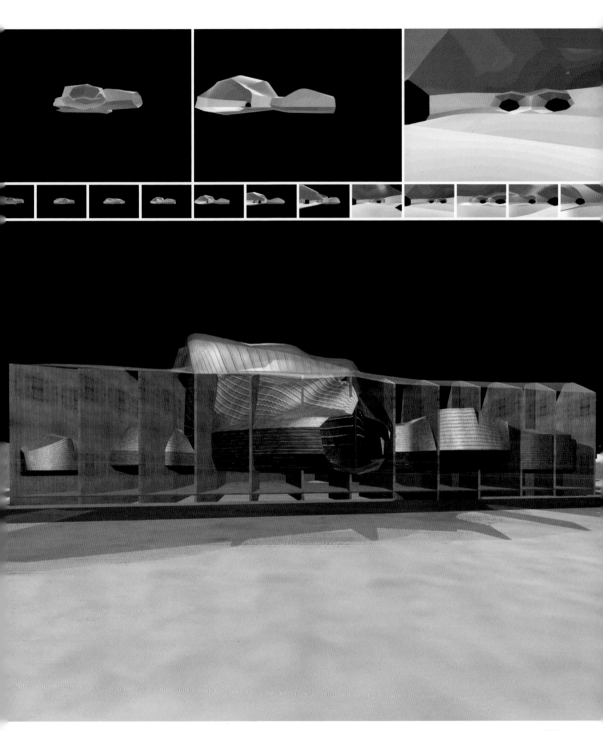

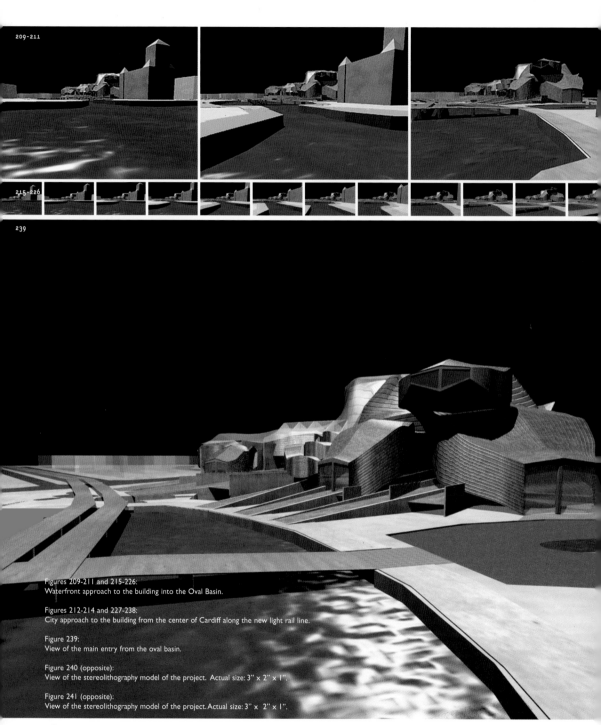

Figures 209-211 and 215-226:
Waterfront approach to the building into the Oval Basin.

Figures 212-214 and 227-238:
City approach to the building from the center of Cardiff along the new light rail line.

Figure 239:
View of the main entry from the oval basin.

Figure 240 (opposite):
View of the stereolithography model of the project. Actual size: 3" x 2" x 1".

Figure 241 (opposite):
View of the stereolithography model of the project. Actual size: 3" x 2" x 1".

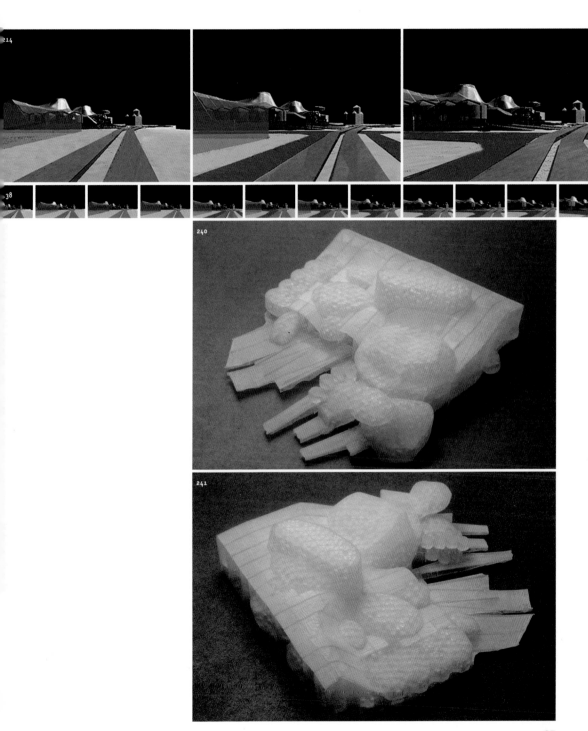

241

243

Figure 241:
South elevation showing entry.

Figure 242 (opposite):
Longitudinal section through rehearsal rooms.

Figure 243:
Ground plan showing parking area.

Figure 244 (opposite):
Plan of level one at entry level.

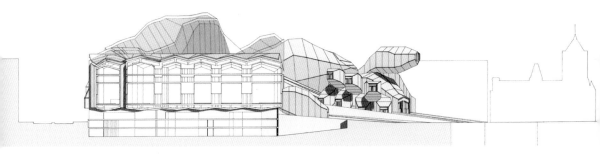

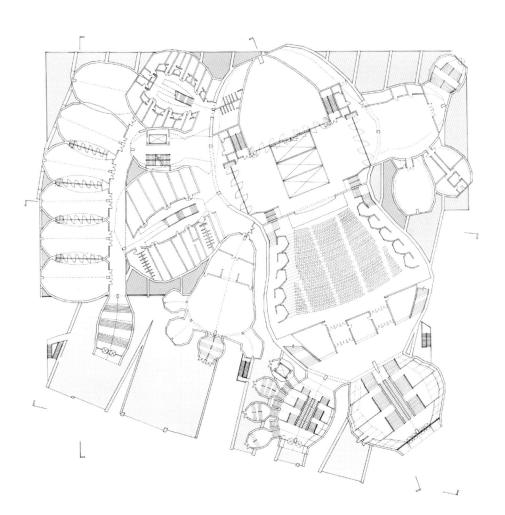

245

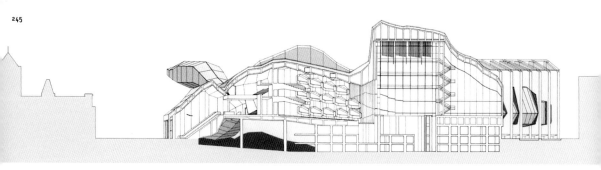

247

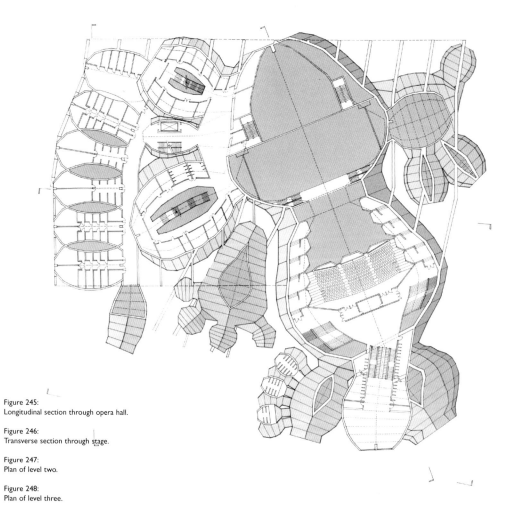

Figure 245:
Longitudinal section through opera hall.

Figure 246:
Transverse section through stage.

Figure 247:
Plan of level two.

Figure 248:
Plan of level three.

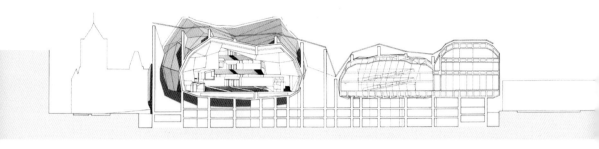

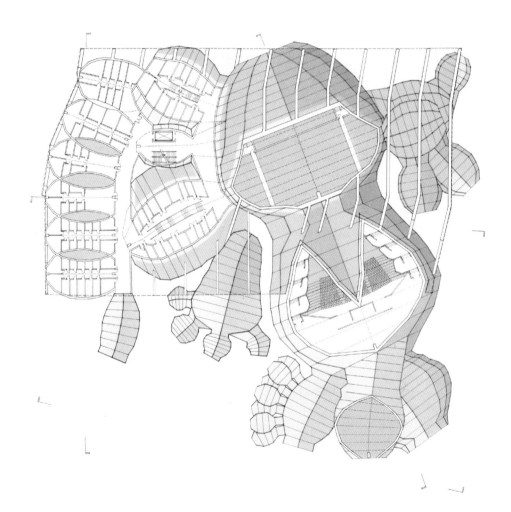

port Authority Gateway competition

This competition involved the design of a protective roof and a lighting scheme for the underside of the bus ramps leading into the Port Authority Bus Terminal. The site was modeled using forces that simulate the movement and flow of pedestrians, cars, and buses across the site, each with differing speeds and intensities of movement along Ninth Avenue, 42nd and 43rd streets, and the four elevated bus ramps emerging from below the Hudson River. These various forces of movement established a gradient field of attraction across the site. To discover the shape of this invisible field of attraction, we introduced geometric particles that change their position and shape according to the influence of the forces. From the particle studies, we captured a series of phase portraits of the cycles of movement over a period of time. These phase portraits are swept with a secondary structure of tubular frames linking the ramps, existing buildings and the Port Authority Bus Terminal. Eleven tensile surfaces are stretched acrossthese tubes as an enclosure and projection surface.

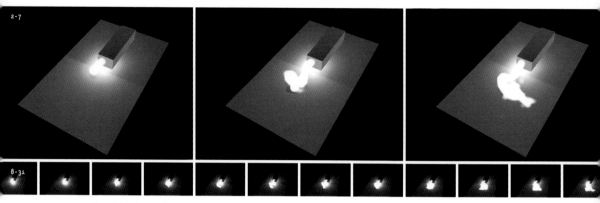

Figure 1 (previous page):
Perspective view of the tensile surfaces

Figures 2-31:
The site was modeled with forces of attraction based on the movement of pedestrians, automobiles and buses. The gradients of speed were visualized with the addition of a particle-emitting surface at the entry of the bus ramps into the facade of the Port Authority Bus Terminal. These images illustrate the densities of particles as they are attracted by motion forces on the site.

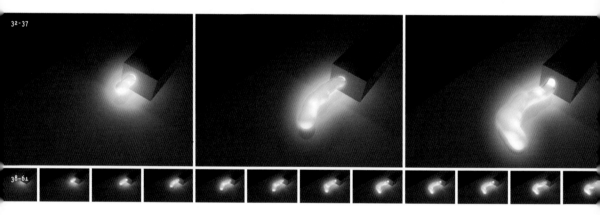

Figures 32-61:
A similar, more discrete, particle cloud massing

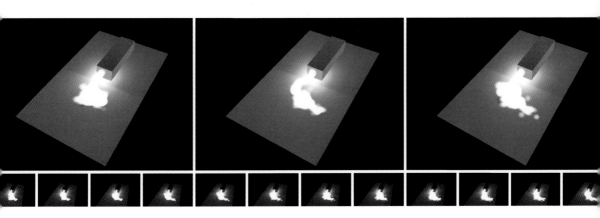

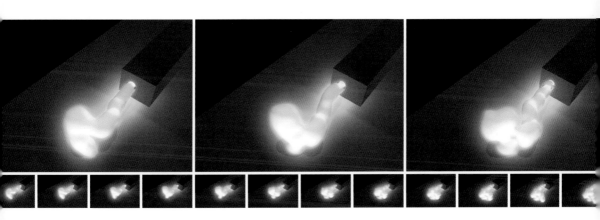

62-67

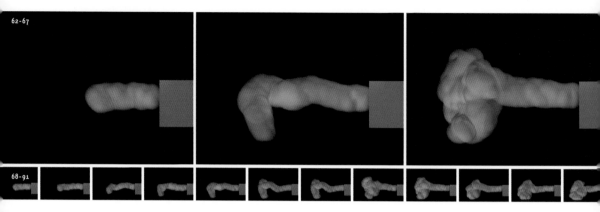

68-91

Figures 62-91:
The site forces mapped with particles that create a single surface envelope.

92-97

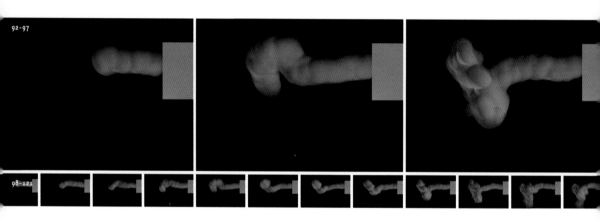

98-121

Figures 92-121:
The same sequence viewed from above.

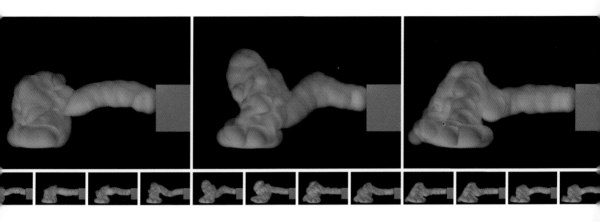

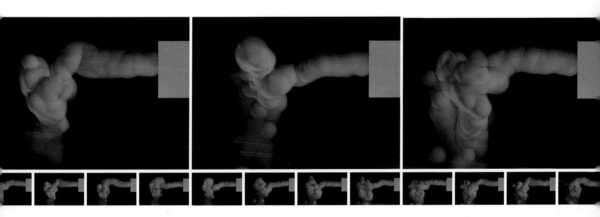

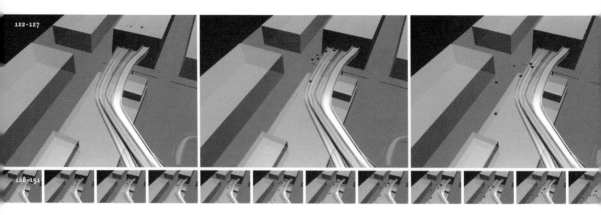

Figures 122-151:
Instead of freezing a single instant of the particle study, an animation "sweep" technique captures a sequence of positions through a phase of their motion. Particles released both from the west facade of the bus terminal and on the street level of Ninth Avenue are the source of these sweeps. Because these particles have elasticity and density, and because they move in a space with gravitational force, the paths take the shape of gravity-resistant arches.

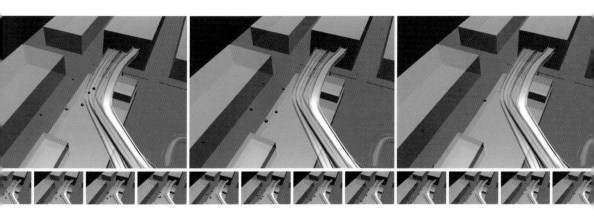

Figure 152 (opposite):
Perspective view of the ramp phase portrait.

Figure 153:
Perspective view of the Ninth Avenue phase portrait.

Figures 154-183:
Particle study of the Ninth Avenue motion forces.

Figure 184:
The phase portraits are threaded by curvilinear vectors. These vectors became the center lines for the tubular beams whose quasi-catenoidal shape was inherently resistant to loads.

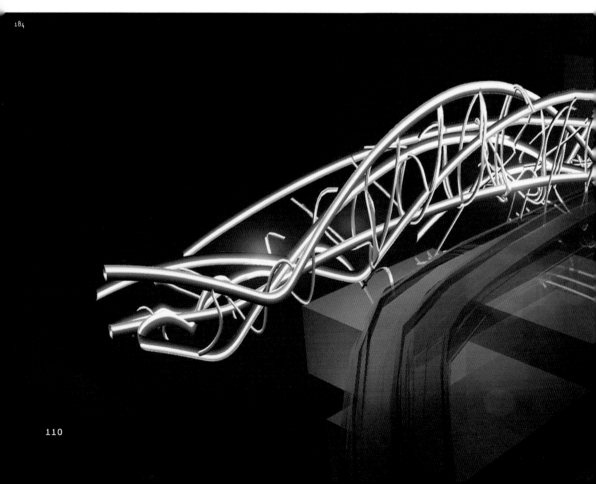

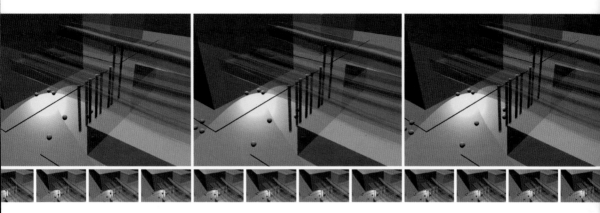

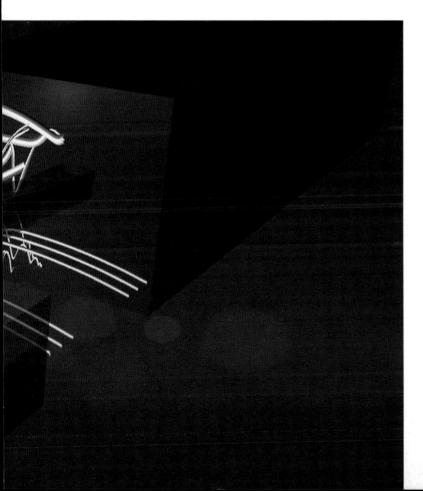

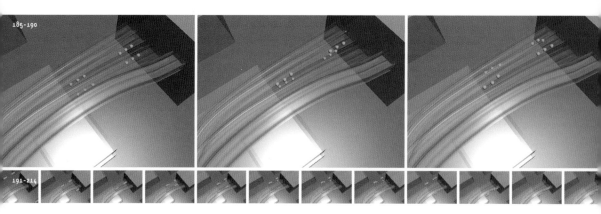

Figures 185-214:
Particle study of the Ninth Avenue motion forces.

Figure 215:
The tubular beams support a series of tensile fabric bands. These fabric strips alternate their structural alignments so that openings are formed between bands. The tensile surfaces provide a screen for the projection of transportation information visible to pedestrians and passengers as well as providing a surface for the diffusion of light from below.

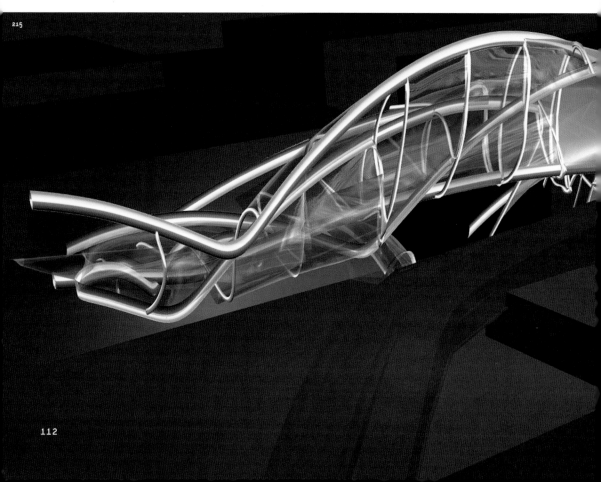

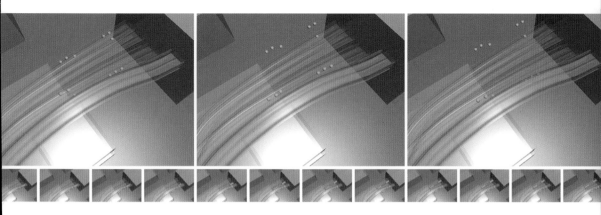

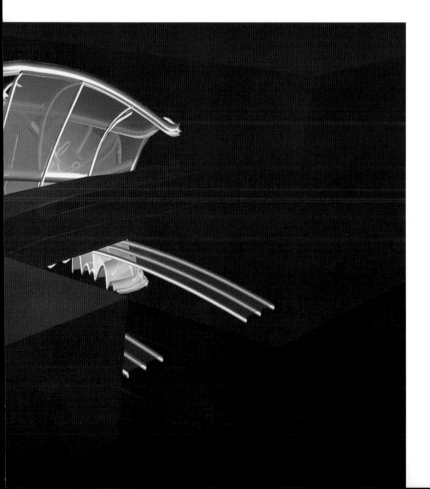

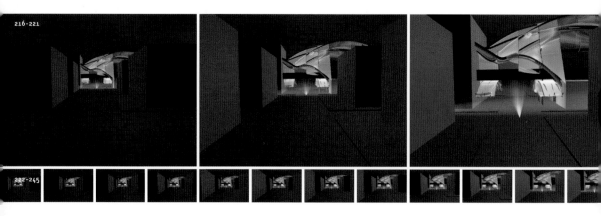

Figures 216-245:
The approach from the north moving down Ninth Avenue.

Figure 246:
The north elevation showing the tensile surfaces that partially enclose the underside of the ramps. The four surfaces on the right receive projected images of transportation schedules and delays. The remaining seven surfaces to the left are illuminated from below.

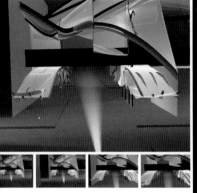

Figure 247:
A stereolithography model of the tensile surfaces mounted between plates of glass. Approximate size 8" x 4" x 4".

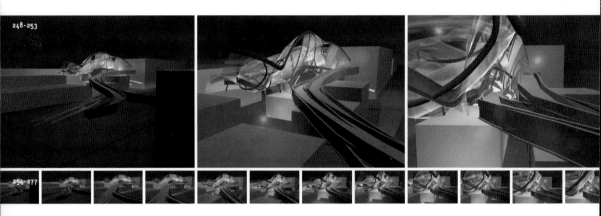

Figures 248-277:
The approach from the Lincoln Tunnel, up the ramp and into the Port Authority Bus Terminal.

Figure 278:
Roof plan view of the structural tubes and the tensile surfaces with the existing ramp structure.

Figure 279:
A stereolithography model of the tensile surfaces mounted between plates of glass. Approximate size 8" x 4" x 4".

Figure 280:
Perspective view from the southwest.

Figure 281:
A stereolithography model of the tensile surfaces mounted between plates of glass. Approximate size 8" x 4" x 4".

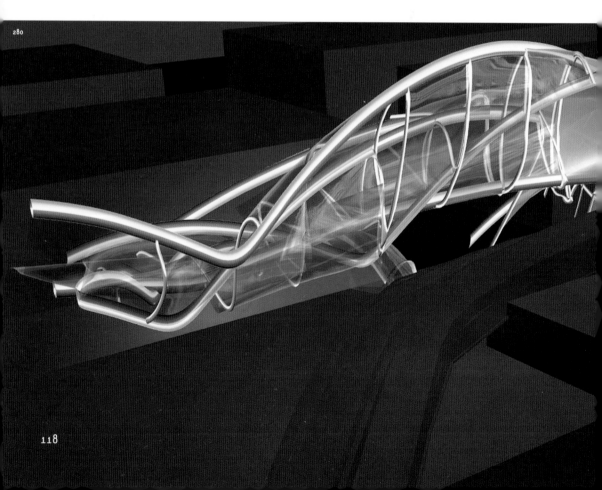

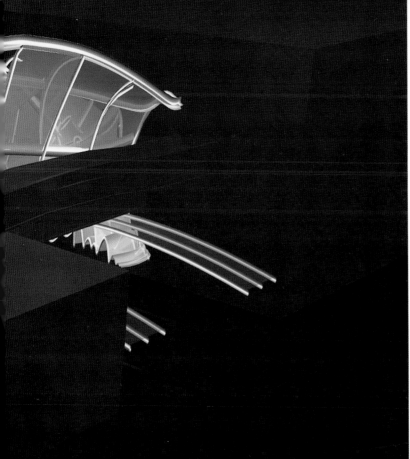

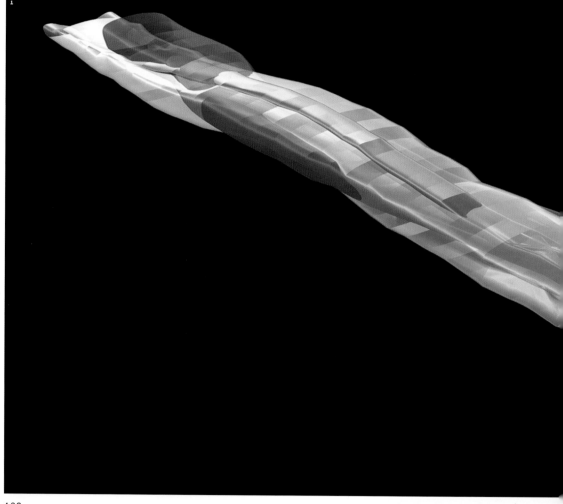

yokohama port terminal competition

The Yokohama International Port Terminal is a location of complex movement and interchange between passengers and citizens, between land and sea, between city and garden, between vehicles and cargo. This project sees in these dynamic exchanges an opportunity to celebrate the experience of fluid and uninterupted streams of movement. Emphasis on smooth and continuous movement organizes the project programmatically, contextually and spatially. While the port terminal extends the full length of the site, it addresses its context by building up gradually at the land end and tapering down smoothly toward the sea. Ramps extend the ground plane into the building, while the garden emerges from the building to redefine the ground at the tip. These transformations are defined spatially and topologically as transformation of the city's surface into the interior volume of the departure and arrival hall (and ultimately to the boat). The surface of the garden transforms from the sea into a passage into civic spaces for events and congregation in the city. These transitions from flat surface to rolled volume pass through each other in opposite and complementary directions. The garden and the port terminal are each conceived as a continuous transformation from interior volumes into outdoor surfaces.

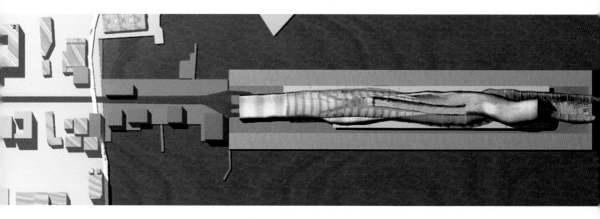

These two passages complement one another along the length of the site as they move through each other in opposite directions. As they pass though one another, their interiors and exteriors intermingle. The combination intersection and passages between these surfaces mediates the visitor's experience of the site, whether arriving to Yokohama through the garden, departing the city and moving to the sea, or as a citizen enjoying the various spaces along the pier. Rather than only moving along any one of these surfaces, the visitor is always moving through and between the two kinds of spaces.

These elements, which begin as surfaces and become interior tubes, are skinned in three materials. The terminal tube is clad in lead-coated stainless steel, as it has the greatest interior volume; the citizens' tube is enclosed with a lightweight tent structure that filters natural light and allows for a more transparent connection and view of the water; and the garden is composed of moss and stone. The structural system is a series of portalized concrete bearing walls. A lattice of lightweight steel members punctuated by cable trusses provides the substructure of the various roof members.

Figure 1: (previous page)
Axonometric view of the programmatic tubes.

Figure 2:
Roof plan.

Figure 3:
Aerial view looking toward the city of Yokohama,

Figure 4:
Three pairs of tube typologies, with the programmatic volume shown in blue and the exterior shell in grey. The first, third, and fifth tube typologies locate the program on the inside of the tube, with the exterior shell on the outside of the tube. The second, fourth, and sixth tube typologies locate the program on the outside of the tube, with an exterior space on the inside of the tube. The third and fourth tubes show the effect of pinching the tubes together into a surface at the city end of the tubes; the fifth and sixth tubes show the same technique on the ocean side of the site. In both instances the interior surfaces of the tubes generate a programmatic "blush" on the outer surfaces.

Figure 5:
The terminal tube transforms from a surface at the urban edge of the site, making a traffic plaza, to a volume at the ocean edge of the site, creating a departures and arrivals terminal.

Figure 6:
The citizens' tube transforms from a surface at the ocean edge of the site, making a public park space at the water ferry stop, to a volume at the urban edge of the site, creating a large donut-like parking garage with an empty center through which the visitors enter the terminal hall.

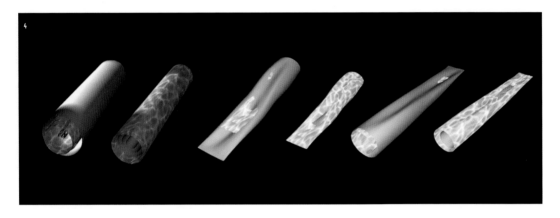

4

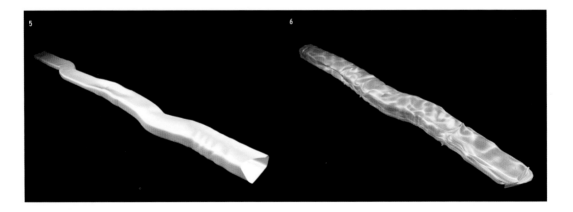

5   6

Figure 7:
The two tubes were threaded through one another based on the docking patterns of the ships. Through the empty center of each tube the surface of the opposite tube emerges, knitting the public and transportation systems as two intersecting, alternating volumes which become surfaces. The red points locate the docking points of each of the boats using the terminal. Through these points a spline was drawn. Unlike a linear axis, a spline finds a curvilinear trajectory through a sequence of points based on the network of coordinates. As the spline used is a seven-degree spline, every location along the spline is determined by the adjacent seven points in the network and its proximity to each of those points. The white line is the spline for the terminal that interpolates continuously as a curve between the specific docking points of all of the boats using the terminal. Mirrored from that spline is a second public spline that occupies the open areas of the site by alternating its trajectory opposite of the terminal programs. This spline is smoother, or less inflected, because it is a three-degree spline, and thus, looks at fewer adjacent points to determine its curvilinear shape.

Figure 8:
Embedded within the public tube is a moss garden. It transforms from a surface at the ocean end of the site into a suspended moss garden tube that pushes through the top of the building to become a roof garden. It forks at the end to accomodate bus and car traffic entering the parking areas and the traffic plaza.

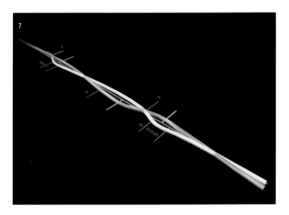

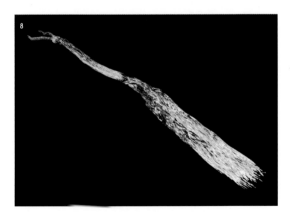

Figure 9:
Roof plan of the project showing the three programmatic tubes in different materials. The Terminal programs are enclosed in a tube clad in lead-coated stainless steel. There is no fenestration in this volume and it is entered from either end of the site as either a volume or a surface. The alternate openings for access and light and air occur at the intersection of this program with the Garden and Public volumes. The Public programs, including parking, cafeteria, shops, visitor lobbies and conference facilities are enclosed in a fabric tensile enclosure supported on a lattice shell secondary structure. The Moss Garden is shown in green, supported by the Public envelope from which it is suspended.

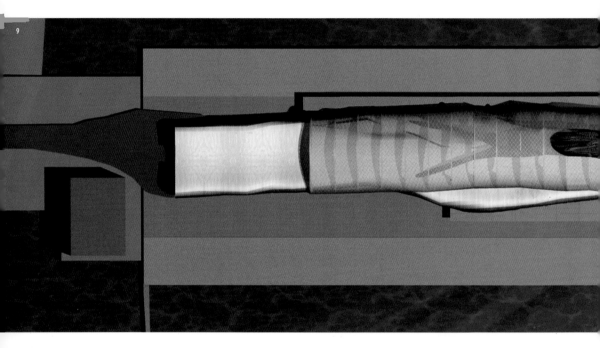

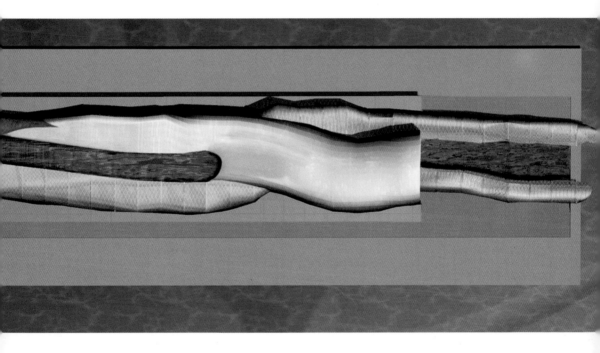

Figure 10:
South elevation showing the translucent tensile fabric envelope and lattice shell intersecting with the metal envelope. The city of Yokohama and the base of the pier are to the left of the image and the ocean is to the right.

Figure 11:
North elevation.

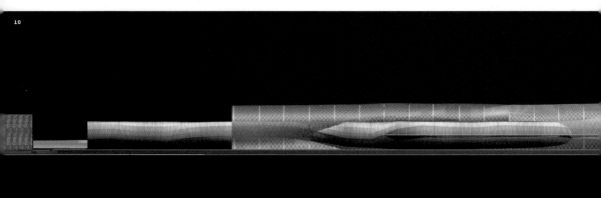

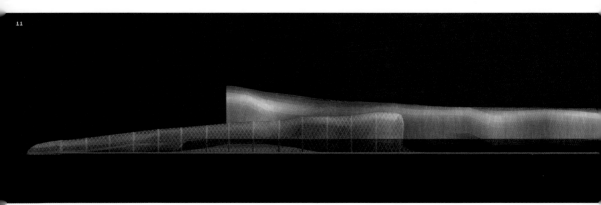

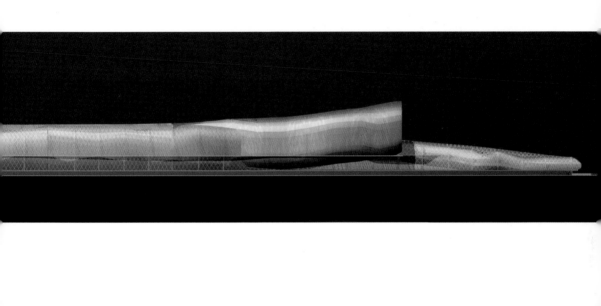

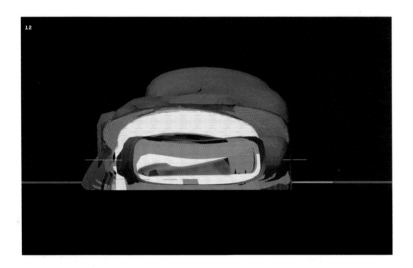

Figure 12:
West elevation.

Figure 13 (opposite):
East elevation.

Figures 14–17:
Transverse sections.

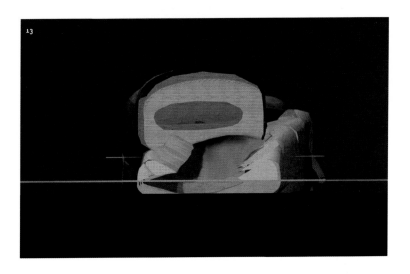

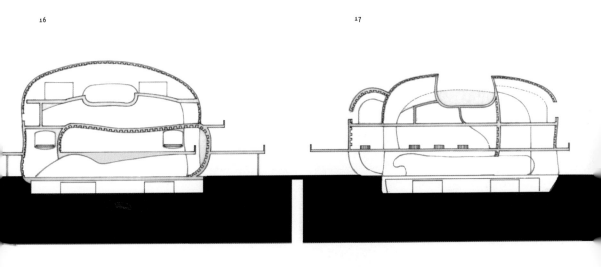

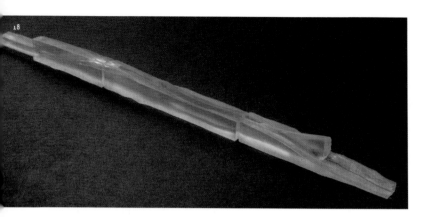

18

Figure 18:
Stereolithography model cut longitudinally through the middle of the site.

Figure 19:
Longitudinal section.

Figure 20 (opposite):
View toward the departures and arrivals terminal from the moss garden at the ocean end of the site.

19

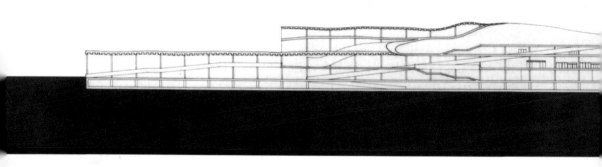

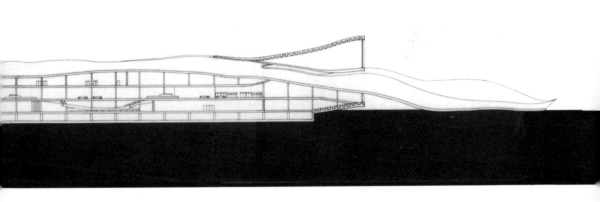

21

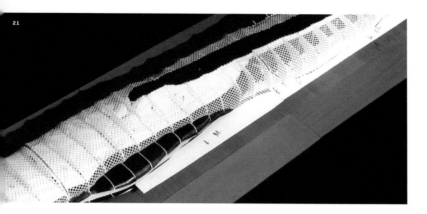

Figure 21:
A large study model showing the structure of the transverse portalized concrete fins, the lattice shell secondary structure with tensile fabric membrane, and the metal envelope of the terminal. Approximate size: 8 feet long, 18 inches wide and 7 inches high.

Figure 22:
Subteranean plan of the lower parking level.

Figure 23 (opposite):
Stereolithography models of the terminal tube (left), the parking tube (center), the moss garden tube (second from the right), and

22

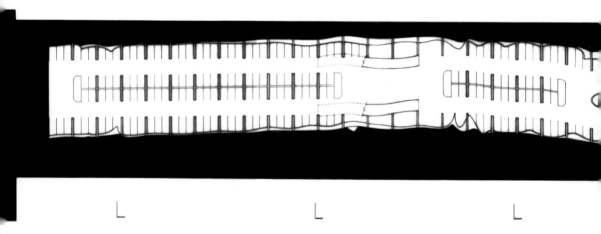

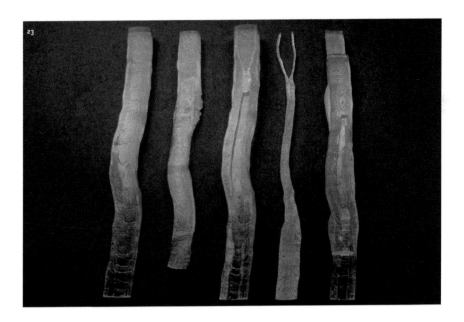

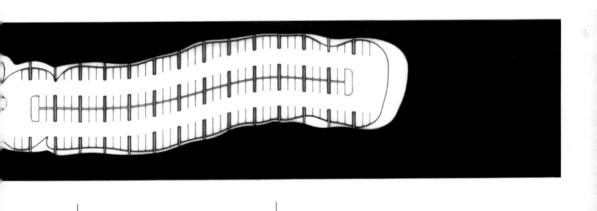

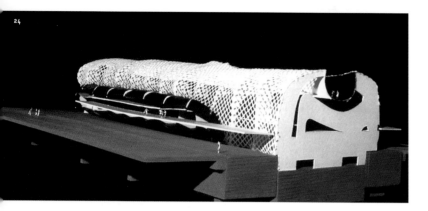

24

Figure 24:
Section of a large study model showing the structure of the transverse portalized concrete fins, the lattice shell secondary structure with tensile fabric membrane, and the metal envelope of the terminal.

Figure 25:
Ground-level plan showing automobile and bus plaza, ramp entries to elevated and subteranean parking levels, luggage handling, sea bus terminal and moss garden.

Figure 26 (opposite):
Laser-cut acrylic sheets showing the transverse portalized concrete fins that comprise the primary structure of all three of the tubular envelopes. Approximate size: 8 inches long.

25

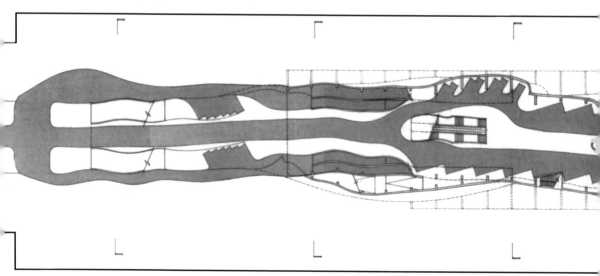

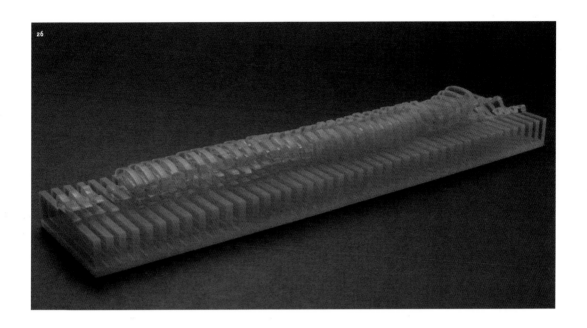

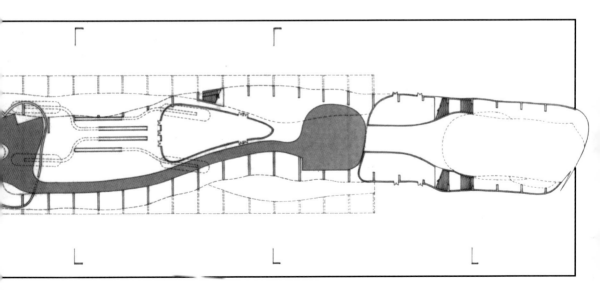

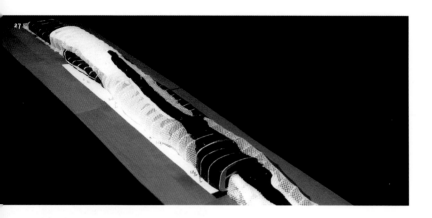

27

Figure 27:
A large study model showing the transverse portalized concrete fin structure, the lattice shell secondary structure with tensile fabric membrane and the metal envelope of the terminal. Approximate size 8 feet long, 18 inches wide and 7 inches high.

Figure 28:
First-level plan showing pedestrian approach ramps, entries to elevated visitor decks, arrivals and departures lounges, access to the moss garden, the continuation of the two ramps to and from the upper-level parking deck, and customs and passport control.

Figure 29 (opposite):
Laser-cut acrylic sheets showing the transverse portalized concrete fins that comprise the primary structure of all three of the

28

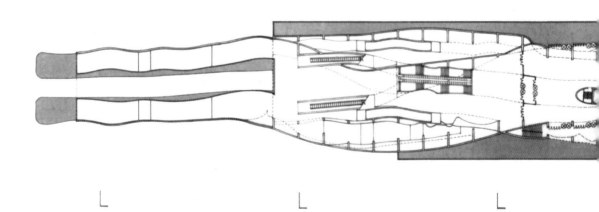

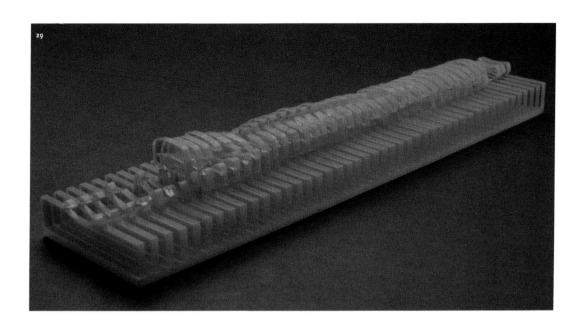

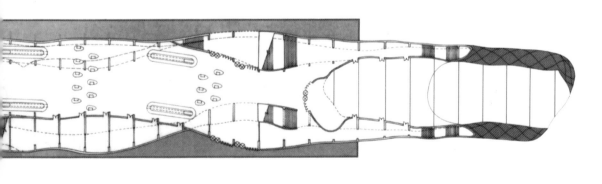

30

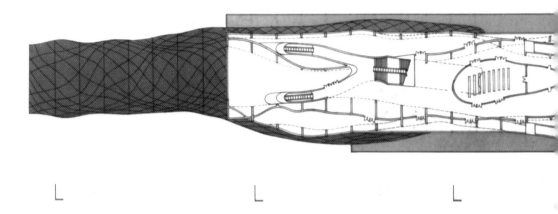

Figure 30:
Second-level plan showng the forked entries to the suspended roof moss garden, the visitors observation decks, the cafeteria and shops.

Figure 31:
Third-level plan showing the upper level parking, the roof moss garden open to the sky, and the conference center overlooking the outdoor moss garden below.

31

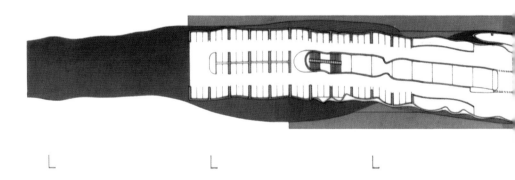

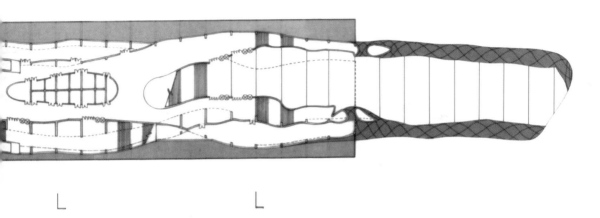

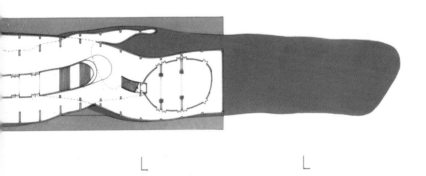

House Prototype in Long Island

The project began as a site analysis for a small weekend house. The site in Amagansett Long Island has an existing ranch house set back from Atlantic Avenue that is one lot away from the beach and the Atlantic ocean. The site is mapped based on visual obstacles and visual attractors using forces of various shapes and configurations. The foundations of the existing house are modeled using a gathering vortex force; the oak tree and the neighboring house are modeled using a repelling radial force; the existing driveway, with a gathering linear directional force; and the coastline with a strong gathering area force. These forces produce a gradient field of attraction and repulsion across the site. Into this field of forces various flexible house prototypes are placed in order to study their alignments and deformations.

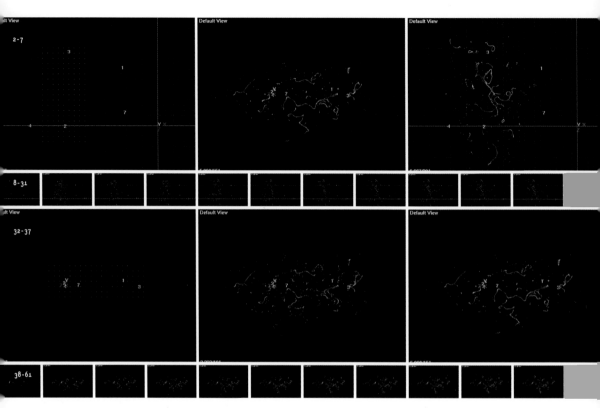

Figure 1: (previous page)
Perspective image of the fourth and final prototype house.

Figure 2-31:
Our initial approach to this single-family summer house was to map the forces of the site. We assigned various elements of the existing site forces of attraction and repulsion, and then mapped the resulting behavior patterns. The elements mapped included (1) the location of a neighboring house, blocking the view of the Atlantic Ocean, (2) a large tree also located in the line of sight to the ocean, (3) an existing foundation from the previous house, (4) an existing driveway, (5) and an existing orchard on the site. The forces were allowed to act in free space and interact with one another in a gradient fashion, as they emanate a field of influence without any distinct contour or boundary. The shapes of these forces included linear, vortex, and radial directions along with various parameters for decay, acceleration and turbulence. As there was no way to read these invisible forces except in their ability to effect objects, we introduced a three-dimensional grid of particles onto the site. These particles were carried across the site and collected along coastlines and edges between and within forces. We arrested the animation at the moment the particles began to repeat and fell into a rhythm or phase.

Figure 32-61:
The same simulation as seen in section.

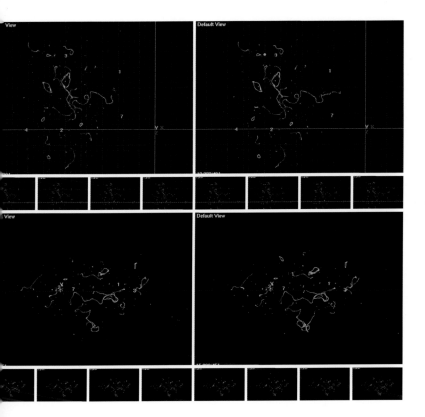

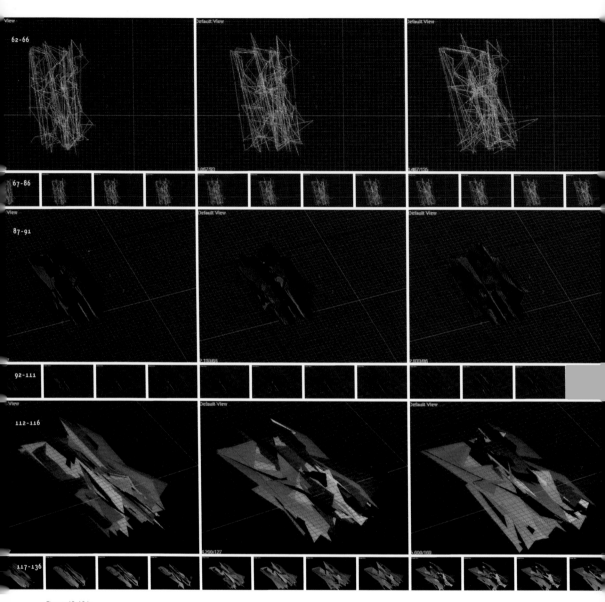

Figure 62-136:
After capturing the particle trails as spline elements, we attempted to generate a massing strategy for the site. This involved constructing an accordion-like surface and placing it within the field of forces. We gave the pleated surface varying elasticity at its vertices and intersections of polygons. These elastic vertex connections were assigned based on the density of particles at any given area. Therefore the surface was more elastic where there was a greater concentration of particles and it was stiffer where there was an absence of particles. This surface behaved in an unorganized and chaotic manner, since the coefficients of elasticity did little to dampen the external forces linked to the site. Curiously, the deformations of this surface shared a general pattern with the original particle studies.

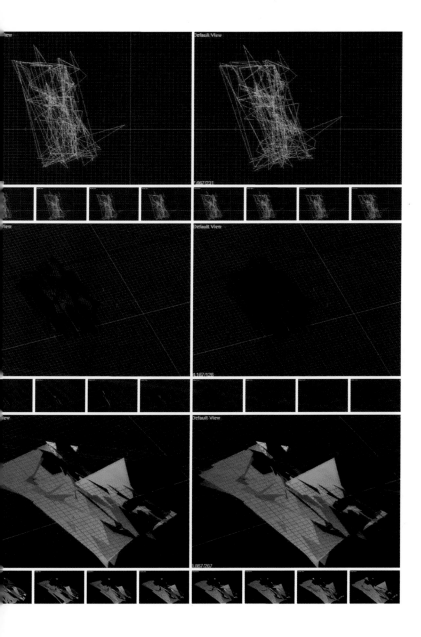

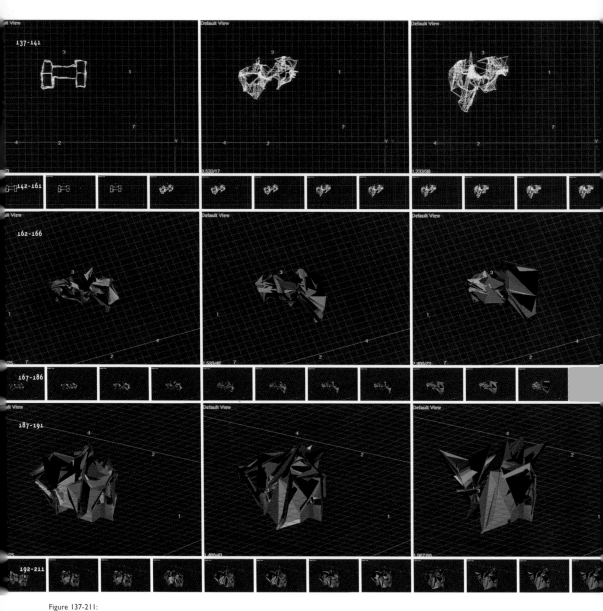

Figure 137-211:
Next, we introduced a three dimensional volume to the analysis. The client's request for an "H" plan organization suggested a main living space with two pairs of rooms at each end of the house: a bedroom and office at one end and two bedrooms for the young children at the other. Similar to our previous investigation of the surface elements, we gave this geometric object elastic connections at its vertices but, much like the accordion surface, it was relatively unconstrained in its behavior. There seemed to be little possibility for creative insight without a more complex and regulating internal system of organization for the house itself.

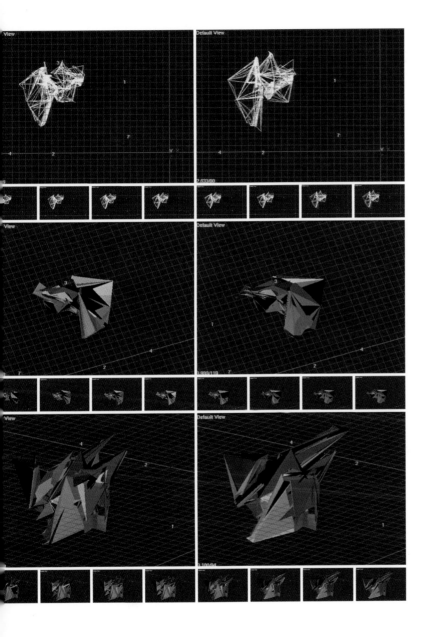

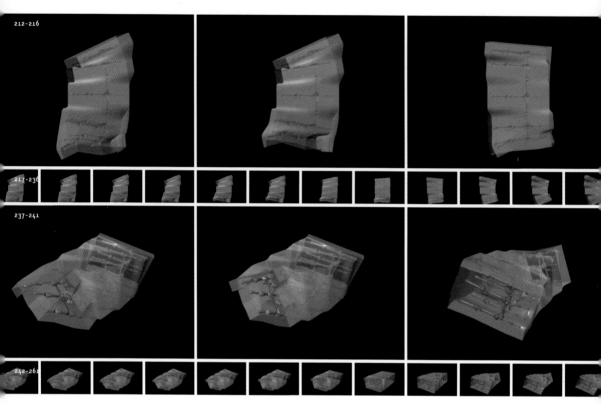

Figure 212-236:
Plan view of the first prototype consisting of a simple rectilinear volume. In order to internally constrain the influences of the external site forces, we constructed a skeleton with variable limits of rotation and variable tension at each of the joints, and then connected it with the animated forces on the site. At each instance in the animation, every position of every joint would respond to all of these forces simultaneously. This allowed a continuous influence of the gradient forces throughout the skeleton. The skeleton is the armature that translates the forces from the site onto the surfaces. This deformation of the surface can also be determined based on specific bulging parameters.

Figure 237-261:
A perspective view of the same study.

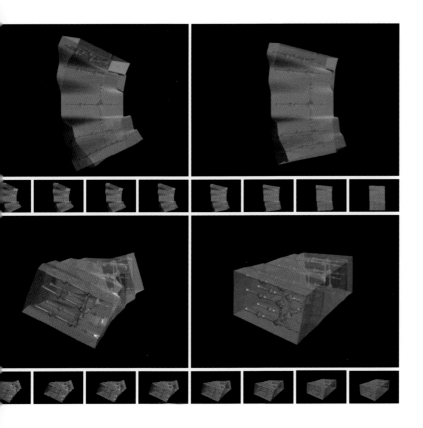

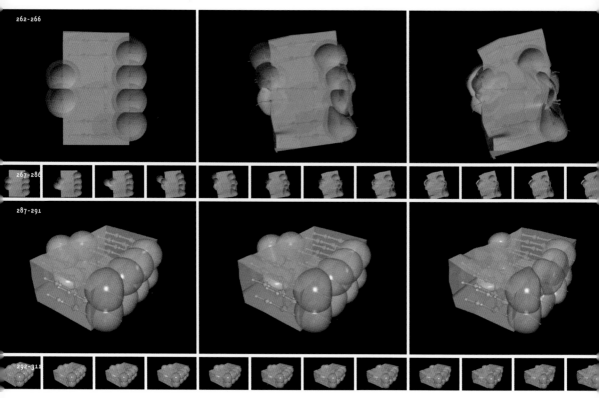

Figure 262-286:
In our second study, we supplemented the simple rectilinear volume of the first prototype by a lightweight tent structure on both the front and back of the house. These tensile structures also extend the sheltered area of the house into exterior space, acting as transitional spaces between the interior and exterior.

Figure 287-311:
A perspective view of the same study.

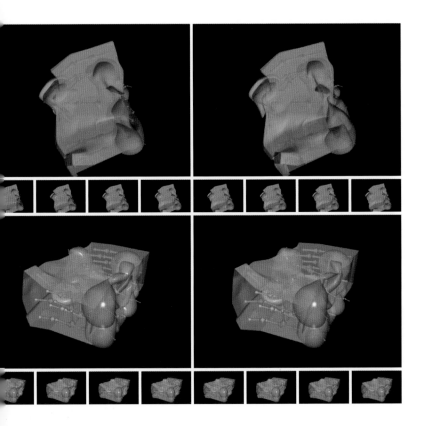

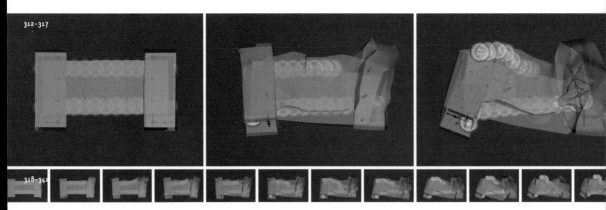

Figure 312-341:
The second prototype is broken down into a main living space with two flanking volumes at each end of the house. Similar to the first prototype there are two tensile structures running along the front and back of the house to integrate the interior space with the landscape.

Figure 342:
A third prototype study with the flanking volumes shifted forward and back on each end respectively. The tensile structures were oriented perpendicular to the main living space along the interior faces of the two end volumes. This plan view is of the initial conditions in a static environment.

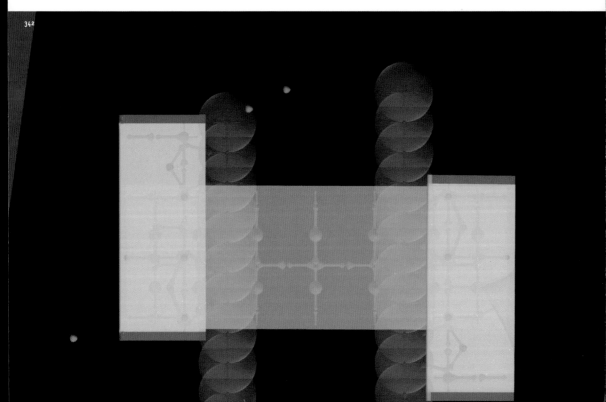

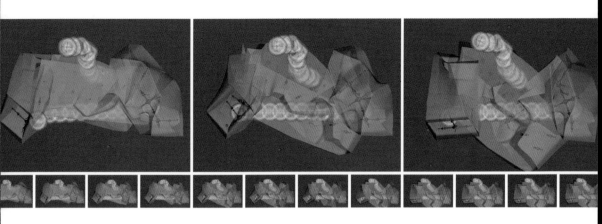

Figure 343:
An intermediate position of the third prototype based on the influence of the site forces.

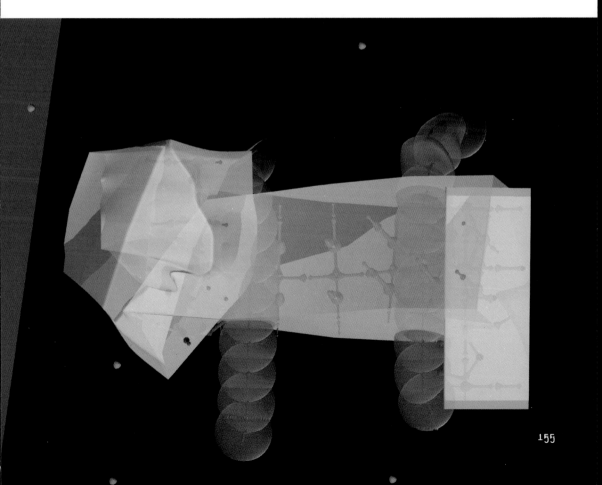

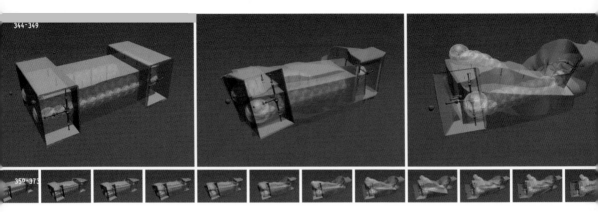

Figure 344-373:
A perspective view of the second prototype.

Figure 374:
An elevation of the second prototype.

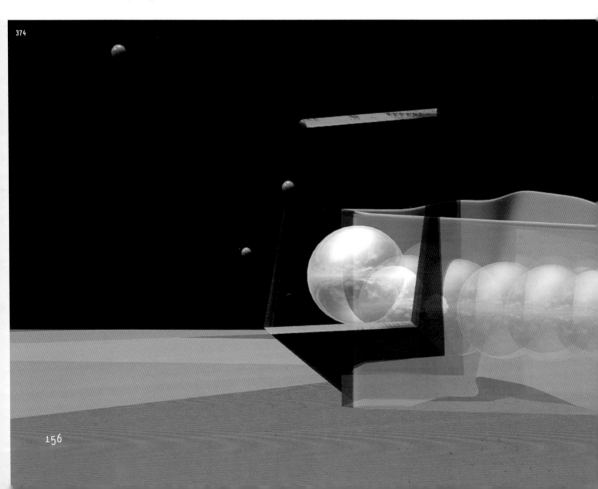

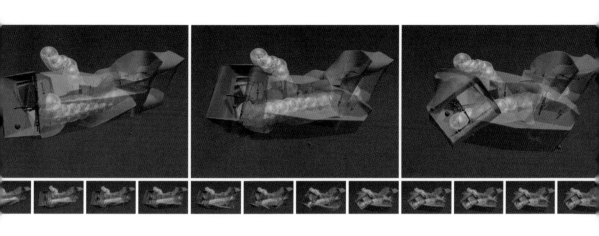

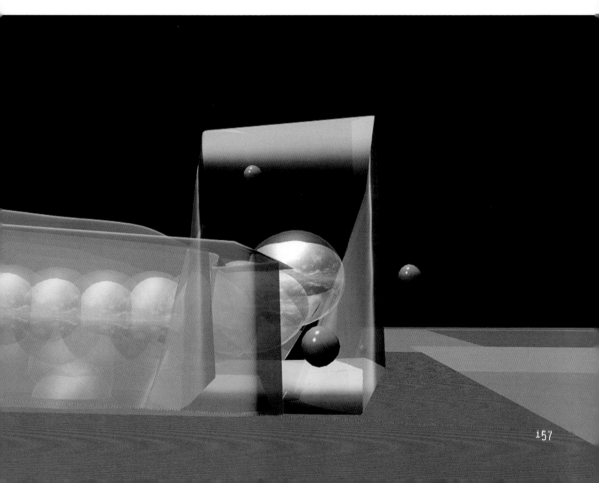

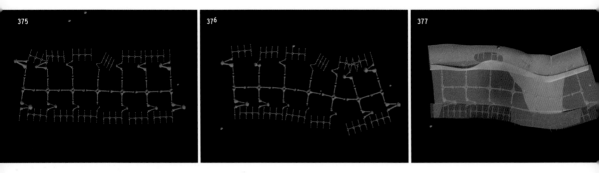

Figures 375 and 376:
In the fourth, and final, prototype, we simplified the skeleton into a linear structure so that the influence of the site could be read more clearly. The skeleton was organized along a stiff line of joints with progressive softness at the extremities. The tips of the skeleton at the ends of the bar were connected to the ocean views and the center of the skeleton was anchored to the foundation and driveway. Images in their initial and intermediate conditions.

Figure 377:
The same skeleton system with its corresponding surface.

Figure 378-380:
Images of the skeleton in its initial, intermediate and most inflected conditions.

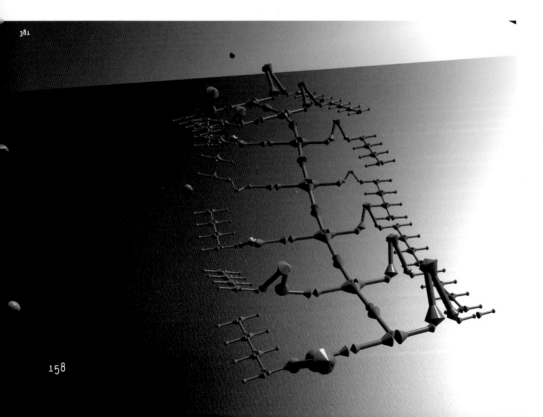

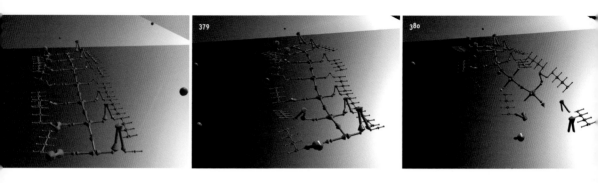

Figure 381 (opposite):
Perspective view of the skeleton.

Figure 382:
Stereolithography model of the fourth version of the house prototype with an intermediate degree of inflection.

Figure 383:
Stereolithography model of the fourth version of the house prototype with a high degree of inflection.

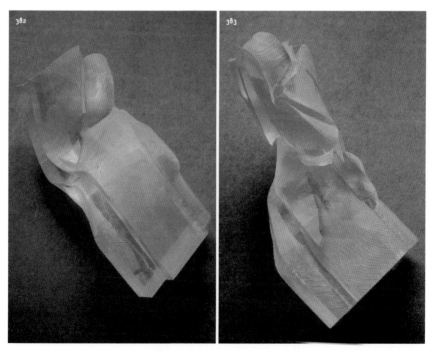

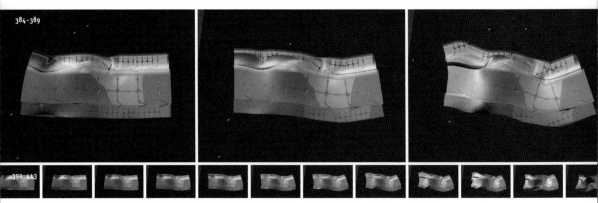

Figure 384-413:
Similar to the skeleton, its surfaces are linear in their organization. The tensile elements are connected to the tips of the skeleton so that their deformation is greater than that of the main living space which is connected to the stiffer set of joints which tie the house together.

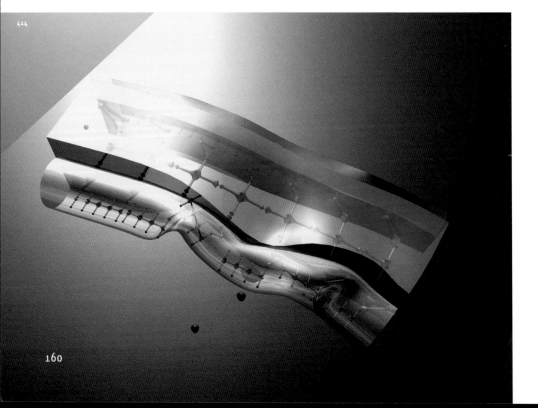

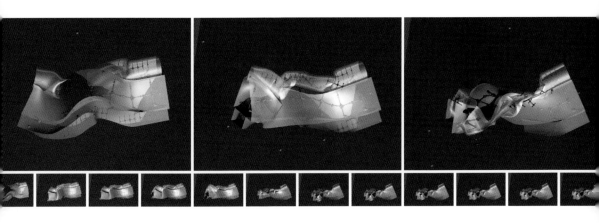

Figure 414 (opposite):
A perspective view of the surfaces.

Figure 415:
Stereolithography model of the fourth version of the house prototype with an intermediate degree of inflection.

Figure 416:
Stereolithography model of the fourth version of the house prototype with a high degree of inflection.

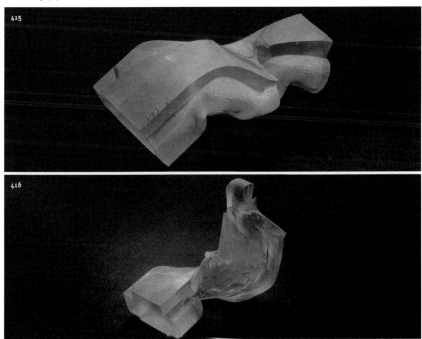

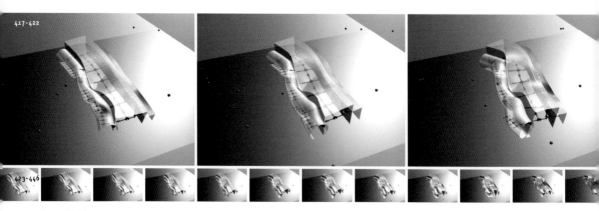

Figure 417-446:
A perspective view of the fourth prototype.

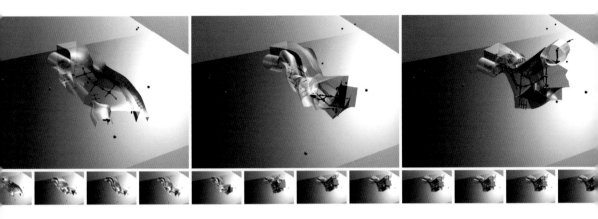

Figure 447 (opposite):
Perspective view of eight positions, from initial to inflected stages, of the fourth prototype.

Figure 448 and 449:
Plan and perspective views of stereolithography models of the fourth prototype in four positions, from initial to inflected stages .

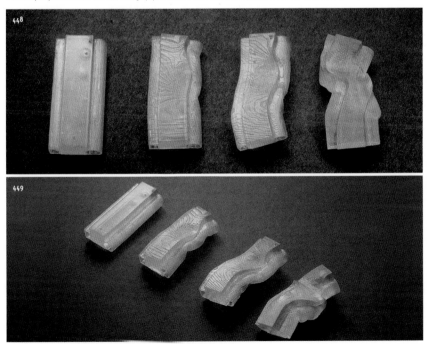

448

449

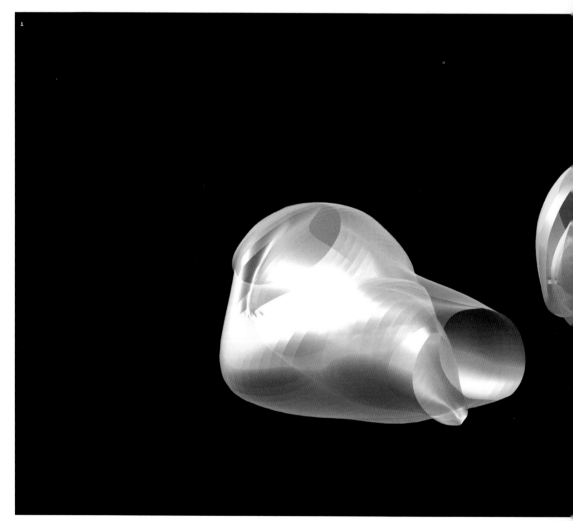

enie onstad кunstsenter installation design

Like the Artists Space installation, this installation presented architectural spaces and objects at two scales; the first at the micro-scale of three-dimensional printing technology and the second at the scale of the gallery space itself. The models are extremely small (less than ten square inches) yet maintain a high degree of detail (within a micron). The same design schema, or diagram, was used for the design of the Oslo space as was used one year previously in New York. Although the design technique was the same, the different context of the exhibition space yielded very different results. In addition to the four projects previously exhibited in New York, the Olso gallery design itself waw exhibited as a fifth project. A similar series of five nodes were suspended in the "keyhole"-shaped gallery and their orbital trajectories were captured to create two groups of composite surfaces rather than a single, continuous band as in the New York installation.

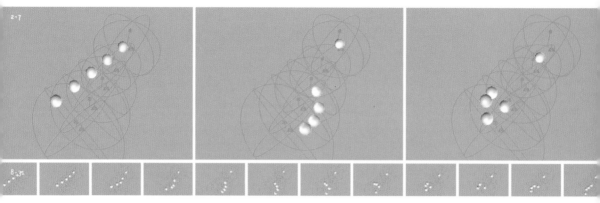

Figures 2-31:
The design of the installation began with the location of five project nodes suspended in the "keyhole"-shaped gallery space. Each element was assigned a specific gravitational field based on the distance to the edge of the two-story opening. Each node was also assigned an equal density and mass. Relative to one another, the elements became attracted with gravitational force to one another based on their distance and mass. The animation sequence was stopped once the nodes began to develop recursive orbital patterns. This animation sequence shows the orbits that develop between the original five spherical elements within the specific context of the gallery space.

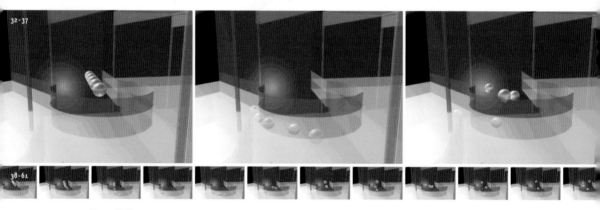

Figures 32-61:
This sequence shows the previous simulation located within the existing "keyhole"-shaped gallery space.

Figure 1: (previous page)
The inflected spherical volumes of the installation.

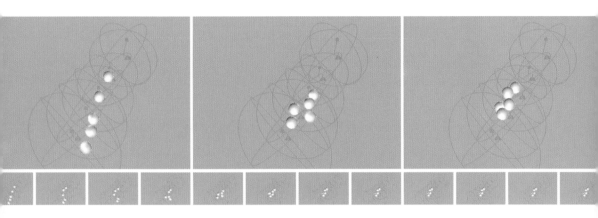

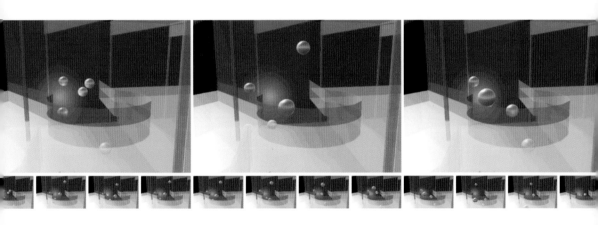

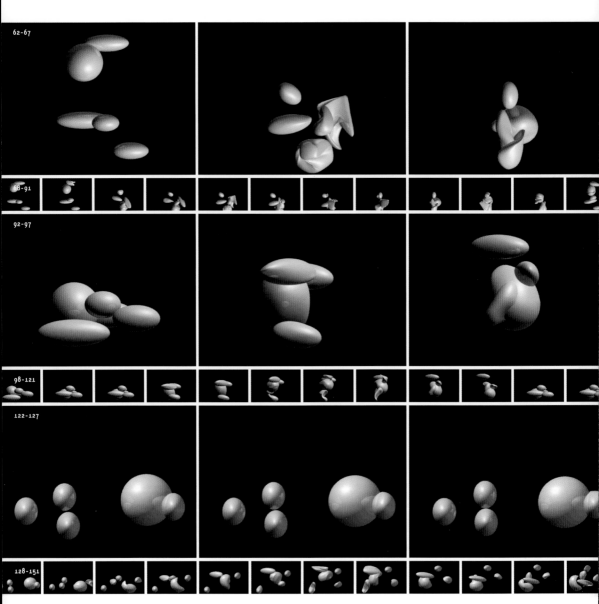

Figures 62-91:
Plan view of the original five project nodes. These spherical elements were scaled proportionally until they intersected the face of the "keyhole" gallery. Each element was then animated along the orbital path retrieved from the last dynamic simulation. The surfaces are inflected and deformed by the mass of adjacent elements and by the flow curve of their orbits.

Figures 92-121:
Front elevation of the same sequence

Figures 122-151:
Side elevation of the same sequence.

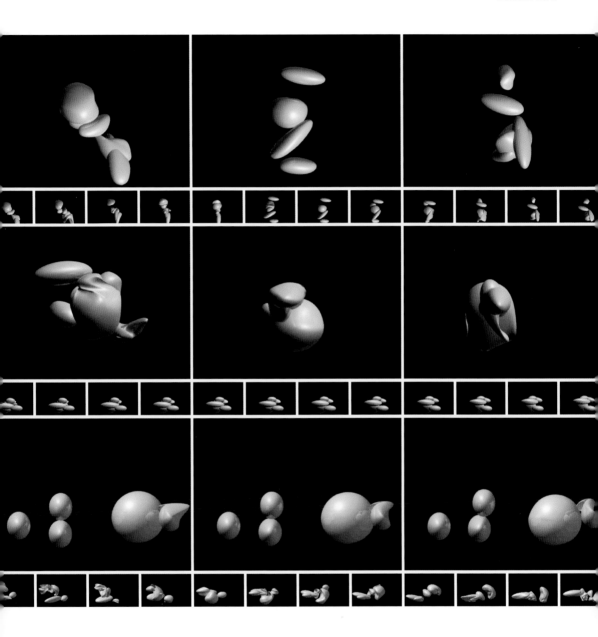

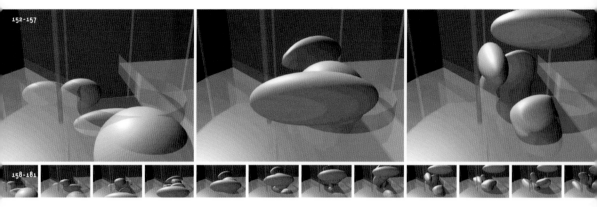

Figures 152-181:
Axonometric view of the previous animation study placed within the "keyhole" gallery space

Figure 182:
Perspective view of the same study.

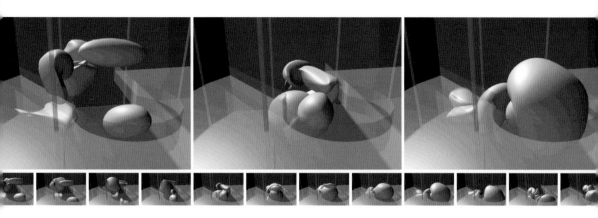

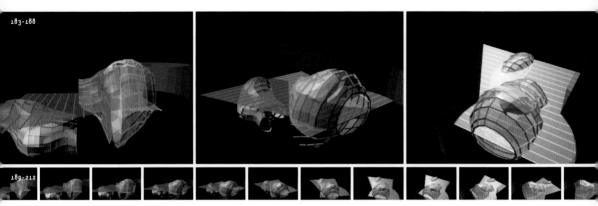

Figures 183-212:
Subdivision of the intersected surfaces of the five original nodes based on a .5 meter bay structure. Linear beams spanning the keyhole opening in the floor of the gallery support the ribs of the bays. These ribs were fabricated from bent bar stock steel and bolted directly to the square tube stock aluminum beams. The beams were post tensioned with steel cables once installed in the opening in the floor.

Figure 213:
Side view

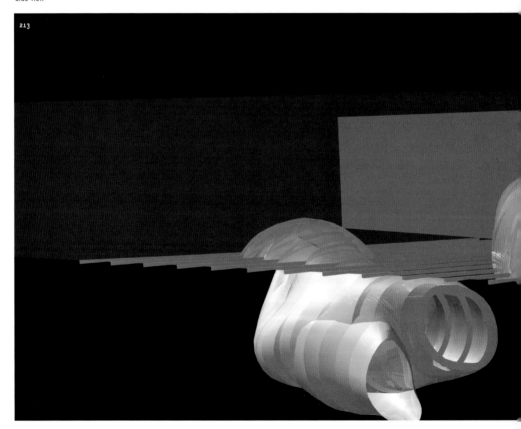

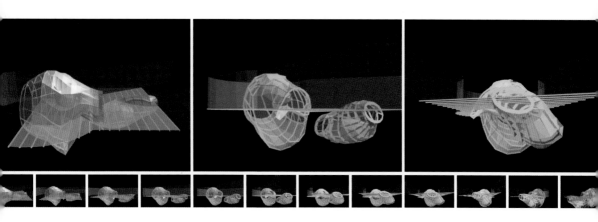

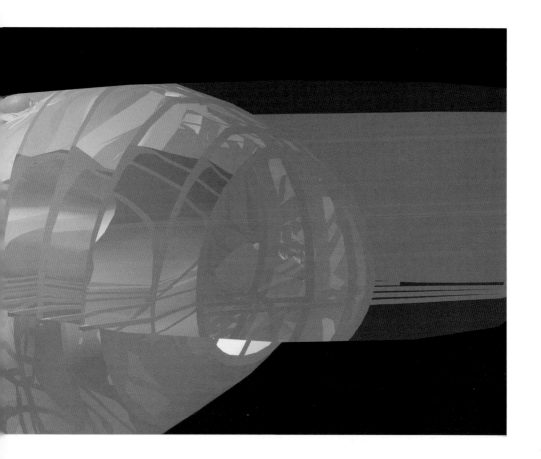

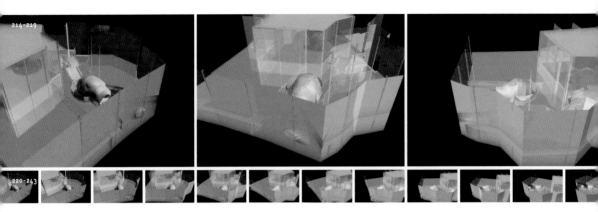

Figures 214-243:
View of the structure placed in the "keyhole" gallery

Figures 244:
Perspective view from above

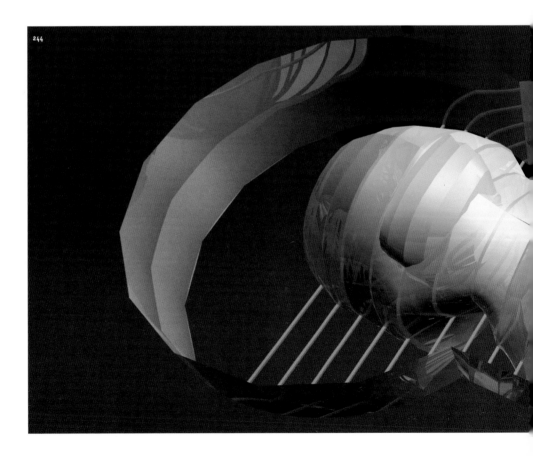

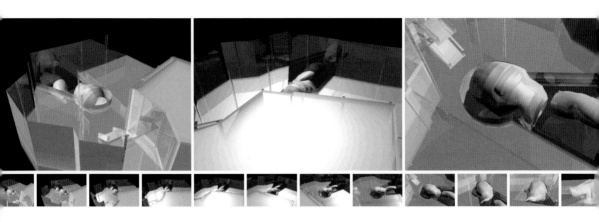

Figures 245-274:
Continuation of the previous animation sequence

Figures 275, 276:
Perspective views of the installation with the structural beams and ribs

276

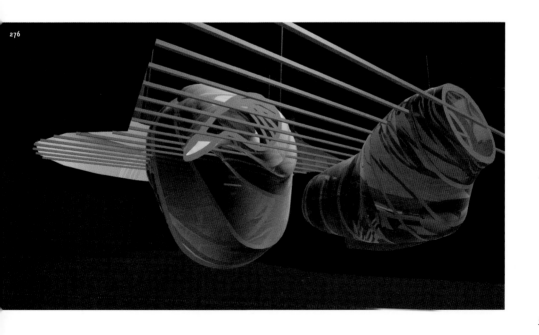

277

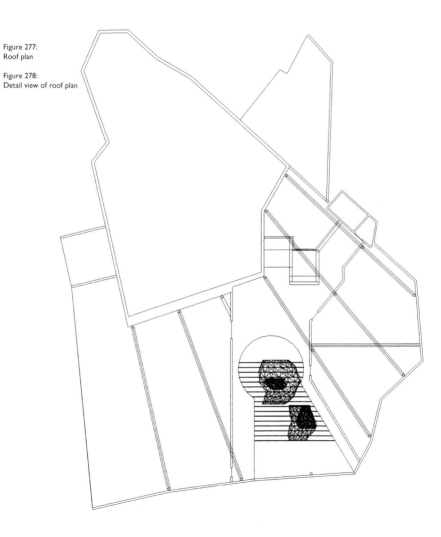

Figure 277:
Roof plan

Figure 278:
Detail view of roof plan

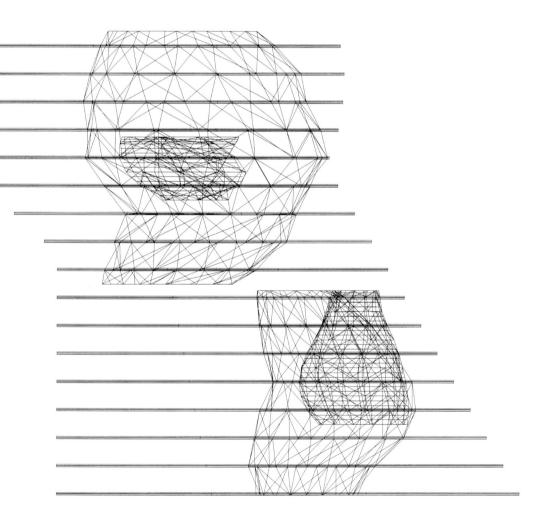

279-283

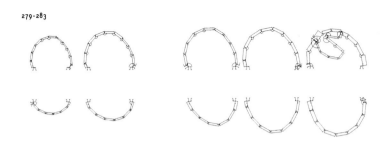

Figures 279-283:
A series of cross sections through the surfaces

Figure 284:
The surfaces unfolded

284

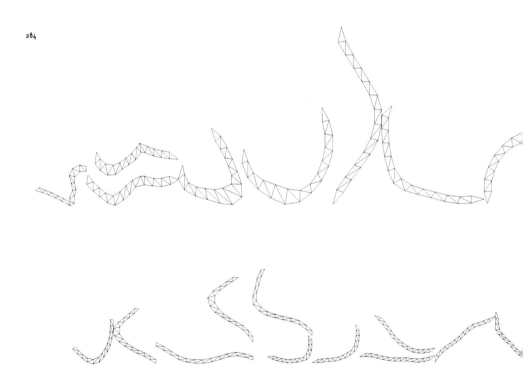

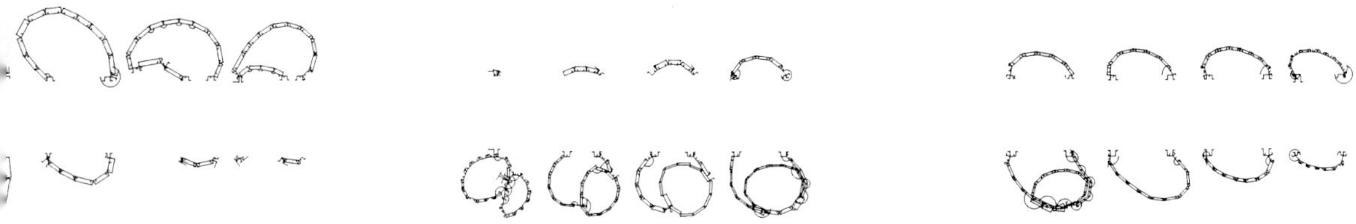

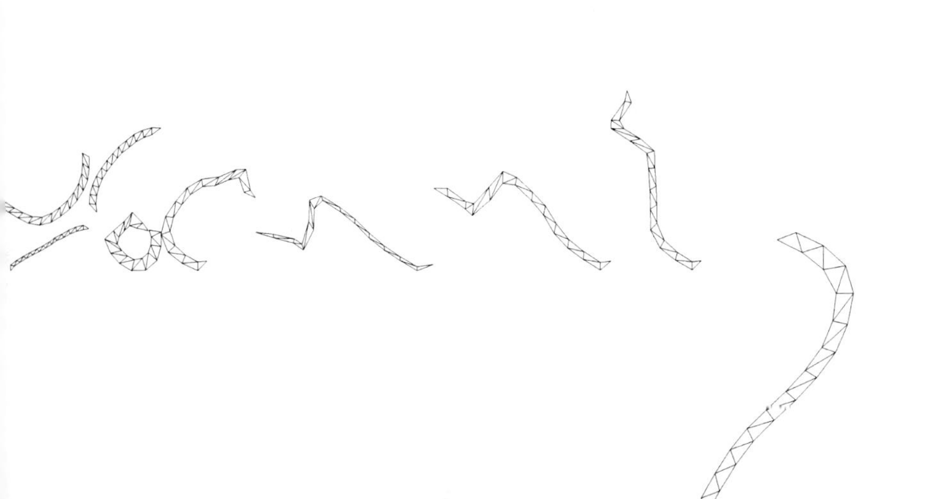

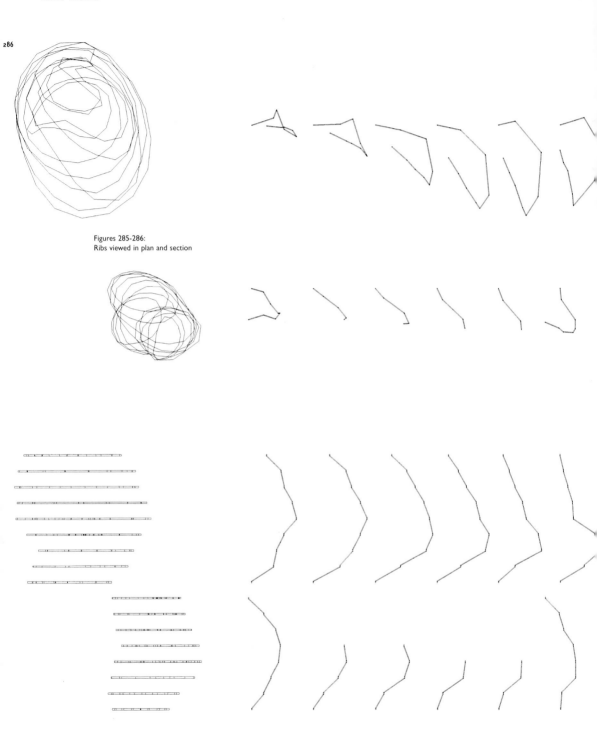

Figures 285-286:
Ribs viewed in plan and section

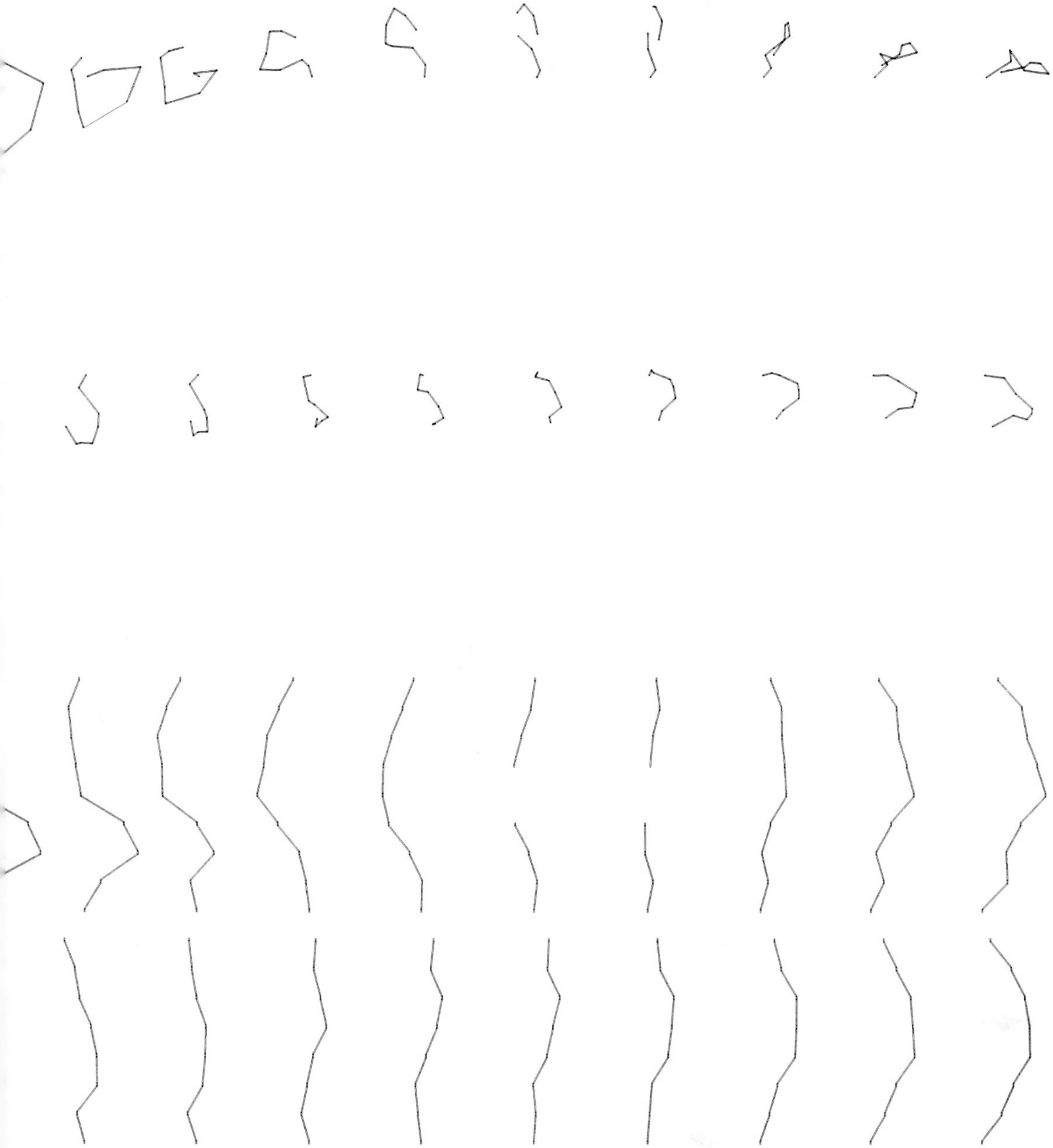

enie onstad kunstsenter
oslo, norway

The installation housed a series of monitors playing computer-generated animations of the design process of the projects, computers where the spaces could be explored interactively by visitors in real time, as well as a series of

model cases containing three dimensional print-outs using computer controlled rapid-prototyping machines. The installation was constructed of lightweight materials on the ground and lifted into place within the "keyhole gallery" where it was suspended. The spans were greater than thirty linear feet The complex organic surface of the installation was realized through a flexible plastic bubble wrap material that stretches between structural ribs.

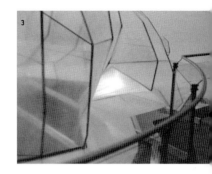

Figure 1: (previous page)
View of installation from the lower level of the gallery.

Figure 2 (opposite):
View of installation from main level of the kunstsenter showing the volume of the steel ribs sheathed with plastic.

Figure 3:
Detail of installation at the handrail of the keyhole.

Figure 4:
View of installation across the main gallery.

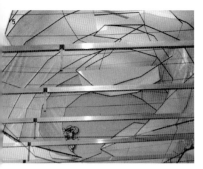

Figure 5:
Aluminum beams with tensile cables spanning the opening in the floor.

Figure 6:
View from main level through to the lower gallery level, where a gallery visitor is viewing animations at workstation table.

Figure 7 (opposite):
Close-up of installation.

6

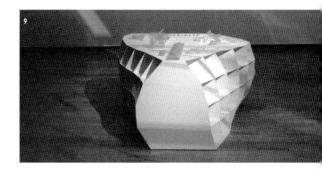

Figure 8 (opposite):
View toward lower gallery entry with aluminum beams and steel ribs above.

Figure 9:
View of gallery table with stereolithography models.

Figure 10:
Visitors in the lower gallery.

Figure 11:
Detail of stereolithography models of Yokohama project.

Figure 12:
Detail of stereolithography models of Long Island House Prototypes.

Figure 13:
Detail of stereolithography model display table.

Figure 14 (opposite):
View of display table.

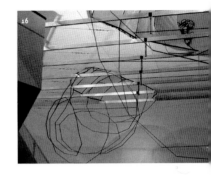

Figure 15 (opposite):
View from entry into lower gallery.

Figure 16:
View of steel ribs suspended above lower gallery.

Figure 17:
View toward entry with stereolithography model display in foreground.

Figures 18–20:
Detail views of aluminum beams and steel ribs.

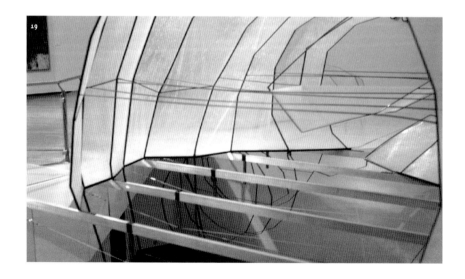

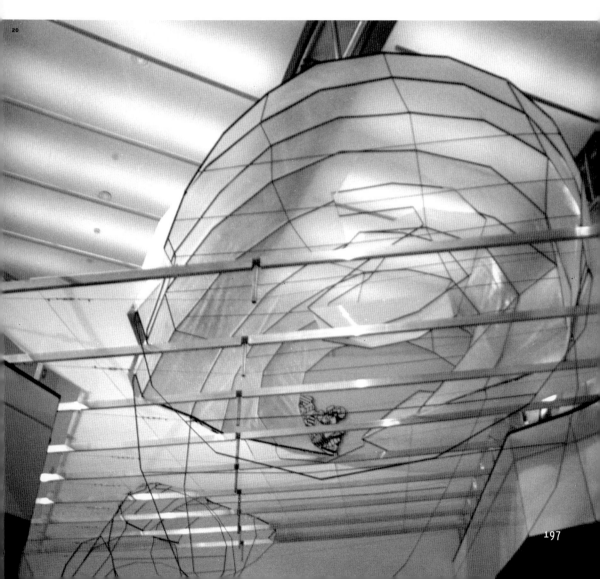

21

198

Figure 21 (opposite):
View from below.

Figure 22:
View through floor opening to lower gallery.

Figure 23:
View from the lower gallery entry.

Figures 24-26:
Steel rib fabrication.

Figure 27:
Installation in progress.

Figure 28:
Welding of steel ribs.

artists space
June 1995
exhibition schedule: 16 September - 28 October 1995

Artists Space, New York, U.S.A.
Claudia Gould, Director
Peter Eisenman, Guest Curator
Denise Fazanello, Curator
Patrice Regan, Development

exhibition sponsor: Graham Foundation for the Advancement of the Arts, Chicago, U.S.A.

computer Hardware sponsorship: Silicon Graphics Inc.

computer software sponsorship: Alias Corporation, Wavefront Systems

on-line exhibition host: www.basilisk.com
video kiosk sponsorship: Plinth-Miko

stereo lithography model production: David Lubliner, John Gidney, and Paul Villanueva, Center for Manufacturing Systems, Advanced Manufacturing Laboratory, New Jersey Institute of Technology, Newark, New Jersey

architectural design: Greg Lynn, Oliver Lang

installation team: Jefferson Ellinger, Donald Hearn, Kim Holden, Noah Klersfeld, Gregg Pasquarelli, Heather Roberge, Ioanna Sandi, Shadi Sharocki, Eric Shonenberger, Robert Vertes, Cindy Wilson, Florian Wurst

internet exhibition design: Ed Keller

cardiff Bay Opera House
January 1994 - April 1994

competition sponsor:
Cardiff Bay Opera House Trust, City of Cardiff, Wales.

stereo lithography model production: John Bass and Ben Staub, Bastech, Dayton, Ohio, U.S.A.

architectural design: Greg Lynn, Michael McInturf, Edward Keller, Chul Kong, Gregg Pasquarelli, Jefferson Ellinger, Kim Holden, Heather Roberge, Philip Rudy, Robert Vertes

structural & civil engineering: Eddie Pugh and Craig Schwitters, Buro Happold, Bath, England

computer rendering and modeling: Ed Keller, Straylight Imaging, New York City, U.S.A.

stereo lithography file preparation: Jefferson Ellinger

port Authority Gateway
March 1995

competition sponsors: The Manhattan Community Board #4; The Port Authority of New York and New Jersey, New York City, U.S.A.

computer Hardware sponsorship: Silicon Graphics Inc.

computer software sponsorship: Alias Corporation, Wavefront Systems

stereo lithography model production: David Lubliner, Center for Manufacturing Systems, Advanced Manufacturing Laboratory, New Jersey Institute of Technology, Newark, New Jersey,

architectural design: Greg Lynn

structural & civil engineering: Craig Schwitters

Yokohama Port Terminal
August 1994 - December 1994

competition sponsors: Yokohama International Port Terminal Design Competition Office, The Port and Harbor Bureau, The City of Yokohama, Japan

stereo lithography model production: David Lubliner, Center for Manufacturing Systems, Advanced Manufacturing Laboratory, New Jersey Institute of Technology, Newark, New Jersey

architectural design: Greg Lynn, Michael McInturf, Kim Holden, Christian Hubert, Ed Keller, Gregg Pasquarelli, Amar Sen, Robert Vertes, Erhmei Yuan

structural & civil engineering: Eddie Pugh and Craig Schwitters, Buro Happold, Bath, England,

computer rendering and modeling: Ed Keller, Straylight Imaging
New York City, U.S.A.

House Prototype in Long Island
June 1994 - August 1994

computer Hardware sponsorship: Silicon Graphics Incorporated

computer software sponsorship: Alias Corporation, Wavefront Systems

architectural design: Greg Lynn, Ed Keller, Gregg Pasquarelli, Kim Holden

Henie Onstad Kunstsenter
October 1995
exhibition schedule: 2 March - 14 April 1996

exhibition sponsor: electra 96: Henie Onstad Kunstsenter, Oslo, Norway, Johan Bettum, Exhibition coordinator

steel fabrication: Alfr. A. Berge AS/, Rolf Berge

steel: Norsk Stal A/S

computer Hardware sponsorship: Silicon Graphics Inc.

computer software sponsorship: Alias Corporation, Wavefront Systems

architectural design: Greg Lynn, Gordon Kipping

installation team: Andreas Froech, Caroline Lie, Johnny Langaker, Kim B. Larsen, Michael Uankowski

internet exhibition design: Ron Devilla

CD-ROM Instructions

The CD-ROM located at the back of this book contains project animations that further illustrate the projects featured in this book. To view the animations, insert the CD-ROM into your CD player, and review the **Read Me** page for further instructions.